Also by Donnie Lee

Hell Is Not a Cuss Word; It's Real

God's Baby
— from —
HEAVEN

Living in Paradise

Talking with Jesus

Life before birth

Future Prophesies

Angels at work

Speaking from the womb

Healings and Miracles

Journey to Hell

Donnie Lee

WESTBOW®
PRESS
A DIVISION OF THOMAS NELSON
& ZONDERVAN

WestBow Press books may be ordered through booksellers or by contacting:

WestBow Press
A Division of Thomas Nelson & Zondervan
1663 Liberty Drive
Bloomington, IN 47403
www.westbowpress.com
1 (866) 928-1240

ISBN: 978-1-4908-4391-9 (sc)
ISBN: 978-1-4908-4390-2 (hc)
ISBN: 978-1-4908-4392-6 (e)

Library of Congress Control Number: 2014912164

Printed in the United States of America.

WestBow Press rev. date: 10/22/2014

CONTENTS

ACKNOWLEDGEMENTS

I would like to particularly acknowledge my grandfather, Andy Lucado, who, by his godly lifestyle, demonstrated what the life of a true man of God should be. He lived a life characterized by love, prayer, fasting, and walking in obedience to God's Word. Though I've witnessed him being mocked for his faith, he never back down and he walked in faithfulness to God.

I also would like to acknowledge my mother who had one of the deepest work ethics of anyone I've ever known. She would get up at 4:00 a.m. in order to take three buses across town in all types of weather and she never missed a day's work in seventeen years.

I would also like to principally acknowledge and extend my heart-felt gratitude and thanks to Dr. Chloe Cummings whose literary skills and countless hours of writing has helped to make this book possible.

Also, many thanks and appreciation to Kemar Cummings who helped in editing the book.

Finally, and most important of all, I'd like to acknowledge God and give Him all honor for His love and faithfulness to me. He is my Lord, my King, my life, my everything.

INTRODUCTION

Most people, who hear my story, if they were honest, would admit that many parts of it sound unbelievable. However, nothing is impossible with God. I don't create the miracles, or the unforgettable events. I just lived to tell about them.

All major events expressed and described are all true events. Though many are supernatural or miraculous in nature, they are nonetheless real. All events described which are "of the other worlds" whether of Heaven or of Hell, are real.

Because of my encounters with supernatural beings and spirits both before and after birth, I have taken the liberty in this writing of creating a guardian angel for myself; an act which I believe is compatible with the events of my life's story, particularly since the Bible, though not explicitly using the term *guardian angels*, does record Jesus' words in Matthew 18:10, "I tell you that these children have angels Heaven" (ERV). Therefore, the idea of a guardian angel is reasonable and commonly accepted by most people.

Additionally, in this account of the story of my life, I have also taken the liberty of making up some minor characters. Some include people like a waitress whom my mother Elizabeth may or may not have encountered when she was pregnant with me. The main point is that my mother was in a stigmatized situation during her pregnancy and creating a restaurant setting and the minor character of a waitress, serves is an interesting backdrop to show the reader the kind of a predicament that my mother was in at that time.

Also, I've taken the liberty of creating fictional names for a few people, some of whom I would have no way of knowing who they are. For example, my mother worked as a cleaning lady for a few people in town and not knowing who her "clients" were, I have given them fictional names.

Much of the dialog of course are imagined; particularly those where I was not present. However, the dialogs serve as a means of relating the facts, describing events, and adding a personal voice to the telling of this true story.

God's Baby from Heaven is based on the story of my life. Some may wonder whether these events are true incidents or mere accidents, the readers can take their pick.

With sincerest and warmest appreciation,
Donnie Lee

PROLOGUE

Whoosh! The little spirit turns his head towards the sound just in time to see the blur of an angel hastily speeding by him. *Whoosh! Whoosh!* Others swiftly fly pass. Something important must be happening. He sees a small band of cherubim assembling just beyond the ridge of the trees in the distance.

He thinks nothing of this all-too-common sight. His mind is on the human children who will be arriving today. He heads toward his friends prancing across the plush carpet of grass; the grass rise and fall like keys on a piano in tune with his steps.

He joins his four other friends, spirits like him, each excited about the new-comers. He arrives to find the group at the peak of excitement because three human children had just appeared prior to his own arrival.

Their presence charges the atmosphere with a feeling of celebration; even the flowers are dancing. Three of the beauties present themselves to the little spirit. He looks at their brilliant vibrant splendor. Wanting more attention, they incite him to look deeper by floating their crystalline colors above the surface of their faces, highlighting and changing hues like a kaleidoscope in a pair of curious hands. Never tiring of seeing such beauty the little spirit accepts the flowers and presents them to the new arrivals.

The children laugh aloud at the sight of the flowers showing off their splendor. The five spirits gleefully joined in until the sound of their laughter rise and burst like bubbles above their heads.

The wind picks up the mirth and carries it across the fields, until it reaches the ears of the five angels that are grouped together. Their expressions are subdued. The Father has given them their new assignment. Frequently during their conversation, they turn their heads in the direction of the five little spirits. One speaks aloud, "Let their hearts rejoice in the majesty of this place. They'll soon be gone from here."

Suddenly, a surge charged with *life* infuses the atmosphere and heightens the sharpness of everyone's senses. *"Jesus is here! Jesus is here!"* The proclamation burst out of everyone's heart without anyone having to say a word. The Lord's presence is simply known. His glorious splendor illuminates the heavens to such measure that it brightens the entire span of Paradise.

The little spirits bask in the fullness of Jesus. His love envelops them. He speaks to them, and each of the five hears him speak to his own heart as if Jesus were speaking to him alone. *"Dear One, I am going to send you to Earth. I will show you things that you will share with others. Some of these things my sacred book has only hinted at, but I will do so to prove that, in these days, you are my prophets."*

The little one quizzically looks into Jesus' eyes. He's wonders why anyone would voluntarily go to a place where even the atmosphere is foul from the stench of sin. *There is only one other place worse than Earth.* But his concerns are immediately replaced with the assurance that Jesus' presence makes everywhere a place worth being.

Afterward, a sense of expectation swirls amidst the little ones. Each recognizes that he has been chosen by the Father and each can still hear Jesus' words to him. *"If you do My will, you will be back soon."* The little spirit wonders why Jesus would say "*if*". He cannot fathom not ever being in the Father's will.

∞

A voice greets the little one.

"Shalom!"

The spirit's eyes interlock with the cherub's in warmest intimacy. They share a special bond.

The angel speaks aloud with deepest solemnity, "I will be your front guard and your rear guard. I will be above you and below you. I will be at your right hand and at your left hand. I will never leave you. I will never forsake you. From birth to death, I will be your faithful friend."

The angel's words signal that special moment when the little spirit's name is called. Without understanding what took place, his world suddenly changes. He is of a new kind of life, flesh and blood; a developing human inside his mother's womb.

His faithful friend, his guardian angel, watches over him in a full state of alertness.

Chapter 1

THE UNEXPECTED ARRIVAL

It's a beautiful day on Main Street in Pulaski, Virginia. People sprinkle the streets and dot the tiny stores in this small town. Charlie's Barber Shop on the corner of Main and Peach Streets is the roost for the old men who come to hover around the radio and listen to news about the war. President Truman has just said something about Japan surrendering, and the atmosphere explodes with bursts of shouts and laughter.

Next door, Mona's Beauty Parlor is also alive, but it is gossip in the air that competes with the smell of ammonia. Old Barbara Corbin's hair is wrapped in a plastic bag to prevent the blue dye from dripping down her face. She strains her neck toward Elaine Hamwiner to hear what Elaine is saying over the noise of humming hair dryers.

Donnie Lee

"Have you heard about Elizabeth?" Elaine asks.

"No. What's going on with her?" asks Barbara.

"Well, I heard …" And the buzz of gossip flies from one end of the parlor to the other.

∞

"Want some more coffee, hon?"

Elizabeth Johnson hardly looks up at the waitress, Betsy. She thinks, *Doesn't she see that my cup is still full?* Elizabeth gives Betsy a slight shrug, which is meant to imply "Leave me alone." But what she feels like saying is "I can't drink your coffee because I have morning sickness." Of course, Elizabeth will never tell *that* to Betsy. Betsy is Pulaski's tabloid newspaper on two legs.

In a town where Main Street is three blocks long, there is no one to dispute that Betsy is the champion of talking about people's business. Betsy has radar that picks up anything that is contemptuous, unusual, strange, or just plain fishy. And right now, she seems to be sniffing out Elizabeth. Elizabeth wishes she could hide the despair on her face as easily as she has been hiding the steadily rising bump at her midsection, but she knows that in a few more weeks concealing her pregnancy will be impossible.

2

Reluctantly, Elizabeth glances up to meet Betsy's all-too-polite stare. "Thanks, but I'm okay," she mutters. Betsy turns curtly and heads toward more-promising customers.

Elizabeth is left alone with her thoughts. "I hate this!" she hisses under her breath. It isn't being pregnant that she hates; it's being pregnant at *this* time. *God forgive me for slipping so far from my Christian morals and for being in such a state.*

Anxiety eats away at Elizabeth. She worries that soon she will have one more hungry mouth to feed. She worries about how she is going to hide her pregnancy from the townsfolk, from her family, and from her friends up in the hills where she lives.

The year 1944 is the wrong period of time for being pregnant out of wedlock. Fortunately for Elizabeth, she *is* married. However, her husband isn't the father of this second child she is carrying. Elizabeth's husband, Second Lieutenant Tommy Johnson, is doing his duty by serving in the navy. She didn't mean to end up with Floyd Turner, but with all the other decent men from town at war, she couldn't do any better than Floyd.

Elizabeth glances over at Betsy with resignation. Betsy is leaning over two male customers and seems to be offering them more than what is on the menu. All three simultaneously break out in laughter.

Elizabeth coughs loud enough to get Betsy's attention. Betsy gives her a fleeting look, and Elizabeth squarely places her twenty cents on the table making sure that Betsy sees her pay. Gathering her little cloth purse, she stands up straight, holds her head high, and walks out of there like she owns the place. No one would suspect that she has just splurged on a cup of coffee by spending the last five cents that was in her pocket.

Elizabeth pauses outside the door of the diner to take in a deep breath of air. She exhales slowly and steps off the stoop onto Main Street. Passing Mona's, she sees old blue-haired Barbara and her cronies gazing out the window at her. Elizabeth straightens her back and quickens her pace as she walks by. She knows that the parlor is like a barnyard for all the old hens in town. At least, they are the type of cacklers that can pay her when she cleans their houses. They might praise her when she does their wash, changes their soiled underwear, or cooks a pot of chicken stew for their dinner, but she knows that they perceive her as nothing more than a hillbilly cleaning woman. She also knows that they would crucify her if they found out her secret.

Elizabeth is not afraid of hard work, nor is she afraid to do what she has to do in order to support her family. It isn't unusual for people to see her dragging a pile of cardboard boxes that she has flattened and tied together. Many people know that she begs the grocer for empty flour bags. A few have even witnessed her taking occasional peeks inside their garbage cans. Times are hard for everyone these days, but for people in the hills, things are especially difficult. There is an unspoken understanding, though, that the war has touched everyone's life from the very rich to those less fortunate.

∞

Elizabeth's cabin looks like a replica of the one that Abraham Lincoln grew up in. It's a simple, one-room structure made out of logs. It needs a little extra attention as she prepares for both the coming winter and her unexpected arrival. She nails old pieces of boards on the inside of the cabin to keep cold air from invading through the cracks.

She rolls up potato sacks tightly into cords and stuffs them into the gaps between the floorboards so that the ground that she sees underneath her feet will be covered, and the biting cold that can come in through those crevices will be less cruel.

Elizabeth has also gathered enough flour bags to help prepare in other ways. She uses the flour bags to make plenty of baby clothes, diapers, and a pajama top for her son, Shelby.

She cans some potatoes, green beans, and corn. By Christmas 1944, Elizabeth has fully prepared for her family. The only thing left to do is to prepare her husband for the surprise that will greet him when he comes home.

Elizabeth picks up the letter that she asked her mom to write. *"Sorry I had to ask you to write this for me, Mom. I wish I could do it myself, but you know me and learning don't do well."* She looks at the yellowish paper and hopes the words written on it will lessen the blow of the news of her pregnancy, even if they do not lessen the burden of her conscience. *"Oh God, please forgive me,"* she says to herself. *"I'm only trying to make this easier for him."*

> *My der darlin husband,*
>   *I dont know how to tell you the kind of trobles that I have to go thrue in your absence. I know that you are fiteing for us and I am writing to tell you that I am also in a war here at home. I*

dont know how else to break this bad news to you but to tell you that I was put to shame by some horreble person. I feel so derty that I dont go in town anymore. I am very scered and I need you to come home as soon as possible. I am also pregnant and God knows that I cant do anything about this innocent life that is inside my belly. All I can do is pray. Tommy, I miss you so much. I am very scered of being by myself. I hope you still love me and that you will find it in your hart to love this baby too. I miss you Tommy. You are the only man for me and I dont know what I would do without your love.

Your only, Elizabeth.

∞

Elizabeth greets 1945 with such a pensive and somber attitude that one would have thought that January 1 was just a day like any other. Sitting at the little painted enamel table by the small kitchen window, Elizabeth's mood grows more hopeful as she watches the sun forcing its way past the weighty clouds. Moments before, they were filled with a mixture of rain and snow. The weather has been as turbulent as Elizabeth's life these past few months.

But sitting at her kitchen table in her little shack is comforting to her. She rubs her huge belly with her rough hands. A familiar lullaby flows out as she sings softly.

"Hush, little baby, don't say a word. Mama's gonna buy you a mockingbird. If that mockingbird don't sing, Mama's gonna buy you a diamond ring. If that diamond ring gets broke, Mama's gonna buy you a billy goat. If that billy goat ..." She pauses to recall the words before continuing. "If that billy goat won't pull, Mama's gonna buy you a cart and bull."

As she sings, she makes full circles on her big belly with her chafed palm. She starts from the top of her rounded stomach, down her left side, dipping low underneath, and up again on the right. Each time she goes around, she makes the circle smaller till she touches her navel and diddles it with her index finger.

She doesn't remember what comes next in the song, but she is certain of the last two lines. "So hush little baby don't you cry, 'cause Daddy loves you and so do I."

Her mind wanders for a minute. *Daddy! What daddy?* A grimace crosses her face. She straightens up against the back of her chair and refuses to think of any unpleasantness. She looks out the window, mesmerized by the sun that has long ago come out and cast a beam across her big belly.

Four-year-old Shelby is asleep in the bed. The possum is done cooking on the potbelly. All is well. A faint smile crosses Elizabeth's chapped lips, and she begins to softly sing again.

On the inside of her womb, the baby is cushioned in warm comfort. He is nestled into the crescent sheet of fluid which embraces him and when the sun- beams cross Elizabeth's belly and into his world, he sees the precious flow of life running through the veins of the womb which holds him. The sultry song outside brush softly across his ears and he chooses this time to make his own sound and speak to his mother. What he speaks is meant only for Elizabeth, and she will never forget what she heard. She will wait sixty years to tell another living soul that she's heard her unborn child's voice.

∞

Around the time when Elizabeth is beginning to think that this baby will never come out, it announces its intention with a dull but distinct cramp that cut underneath her midsection.

On her way to the hospital, her contractions rapidly follow one another like lightning in a summer storm. "Augh!" she grunts, drawing both lips tightly between her teeth. She hasn't been past the diner in the last three months, and now the sign blinking outside is a blur as she zooms past it in the back seat of a clunking automobile. Her friend Sally had asked her new boyfriend, Charlie, to drive them to the hospital. Elizabeth scrunches her face in response to another fiery contraction and grabs on to Sally while the car chugs and clunks in its attempt to speed down Main Street.

∞

Elizabeth is not the only one in labor. A little red-faced miracle emerges after struggling and succumbing to the ordeal of his bones and tissues being squeezed through a portal that, under normal circumstances, is not wide enough to hold his tiniest finger.

Smack! The blow registers through every nerve in the little one's newborn body. Shockwaves of pain shoot from his wrinkly little bottom then erupt throughout his tiny extremities. He screams out! To him, the squeezing and crushing which he experienced on his journey out into this world was a traumatic enough experience. Had he known that this greeting upon his rear was to be one of the kinder experiences of his life, he would have cursed the day of his birth, his mother, his father, and especially the doctor who walloped him.

Soon, cleaned and bundled up in new hospital blankets, he takes his first look into the face of a woman who appears like she alone knows and understands the gravity of his journey – and he is comforted.

∞

Elizabeth has been put through the wringer of shame by the people in her town. The news of the war is not nearly as interesting to them as how she had gotten pregnant, and by whom. She will never tell them about Floyd. She'll rather die than tell a living soul, including this baby boy that the nurse has just placed in her arms.

She names him Don Lee Lucado. Lucado is her maiden name. Floyd doesn't want his name attached to this baby. He is a married man. She dares not put Johnson, her husband's name, on his birth certificate either. Things are already out in the open. Yes, Lucado will have to do. She hopes that Tommy will permit the child to use the name Johnson in order to save him from being stigmatized as a bastard.

February 13, 1945 is a momentous day for Elizabeth. She has given birth to her second child, and despite the circumstances, she welcomes his arrival.

Chapter 2

LEFT UNHARMED

Despite a cloud of suspicion, Elizabeth continues to go to Barbara Corbin's and Elaine Hamwiner's houses to clean. She also does some "nursing" for one or two other senior citizens whom Barbara often describes as her "dearest friends in the world." Elizabeth tolerates working for Barbara and her cronies because she needs their money. She knows that they don't like her because they think that she is adulterous and "loose" for having a baby by a man whom the townsfolk are still trying to discover.

Most of the time when Elizabeth has to work, Sally comes over to look after Don and Shelby. Sally's boyfriend, Charlie, uses these opportunities to visit. Elizabeth doesn't mind Sally having a boyfriend; it just seems to her that he is more in love with his 1928 Ford Model A Roadster than he is with Sally.

Almost every time she sees him, he is rubbing the car's faded green paint so he can see his reflection in it. When he isn't polishing his car, he is using old newspapers to clean the large square windows and the giant rectangular windshield. Once, Elizabeth caught him using one of her flour bags to wipe down the car's weather-beaten soft-top roof. Nonetheless, Charlie's car has come through for her more times than she likes to admit.

∞

Today is one day that Elizabeth is glad that Charlie is hanging around. It is a great day to go for a drive. The wind is waving the smell of honeysuckle into the air. Golden-rods are flitting in the breeze like little yellow wands, and the apple tree on the side of the cabin is covered with white blossoms. Charlie and his car are visiting Sally but Elizabeth has plans for better use of Charlie's time.

"Charlie, you don't mind driving down to the M & P. Do you?" Elizabeth puts her arm around Sally's shoulders and gives Charlie a wide smile. Sally, who loves showing off her boyfriend's car, encourages Charlie.

"Yeah, Charlie, let's drive real slow and show these people that we ain't hicks."

Charlie is all for this little excursion. He leans his tall lanky body against the hood of the car and crosses his gangly legs. He takes a deep drag from his cigarette and gives the girls a flirtatious Gary-Cooper smile.

"Okay girls, we can go, but hurry up cuz daylight's a-burning."

Within half hour, Charlie is more anxious to get going than Elizabeth.

"Come on, gals!" Charlie urges.

Elizabeth watches him as he pours more moonshine into one of her tin cups. "Charlie, what's the rush? Just wait a little while longer. I have to get the baby ready." She quickly put the newest flour sack dress on Don.

Charlie is still holding Elizabeth's cup as he walks around to close her car door. Elizabeth notices that he has a little John-Wayne swagger in his step. *That moonshine makes him mighty confident of himself,* she reasons.

Sally sits in the front seat. "Come on, Liz, we gotta go," she declares impatiently.

"Hold your horses Sal, just let me get myself situated here." Elizabeth lays her fat purse on the seat. She shifts her bottom to get comfortable, nestles little Don on her lap, and then folds her arms securely around him.

"Sally," Elizabeth begins, "I want to stop at the M & P and see if I can get some more bags. The baby needs more diapers and I got to make him another dress." She knows that a flour-bag dress is the best thing to put on a little baby even if it is a boy; it's easier to change his diaper that way. Elizabeth begins going over all the things that she wants to buy at the M & P. "I hope they have some fat-back this week. Whoever heard of a store not having fat-back? Remind me to pick that up too. Okay?"

Sally isn't paying attention. She is listening to the radio and softly humming *Rum and Coca Cola* along with the Andrews Sisters. Charlie decides to holler back an answer to Elizabeth. He starts to say "Okay" but all that comes out of his mouth is "O". The horse and buggy in front of him cut his word short.

Driving the maximum speed of 25 miles per hour down an incline in a thousand-pound machine of iron and steel is an invitation for disaster, especially when the driver is one in Charlie's inebriated condition. The car swerves pass the horse, before nose-diving down an embankment and into a tree.

The impact ejects Elizabeth and her baby through the soft roof of the Model-A like two marbles flung loose from a sling shot.

∞

The shock of such an unexpected calamity can take the body and mind into a maze of confusion, but Elizabeth's mind clearly registers two things. The first is her baby. The second is seeing her arms empty.

"Don? Don!"

A sick feeling grabs hold of her. She gets up off the ground as if she was not in an accident and thrown several feet in the air.

"Don!" she cries out as her eyes dart amidst the trees by the road side.

"Don! Don!"

In shock, a disoriented Elizabeth staggers around, blinded by tears. Within moments, she hears his cry. It's such a terrible sound that it breaks her heart all over again.

Elizabeth rushes toward the direction of Don's cry. "Thank you, Jesus. Thank you, Jesus. Thank you, Jesus." She repeats these words like a mantra because somewhere in her mind it registers that only *living* babies cry. She moves swiftly toward a section of overgrown bushes, tripping several times over rocks and branches, before stopping short at the mouth of a ten-foot drop. Rocks and boulders are all she sees down the side of the hill. She reasons that her baby must have hit his head on one of them, but his crying tells her that he is alive.

"Oh God! Oh God! Oh God!" She wails this prayer to God, thankful for her son being alive. Yet, she is also hoping that he is not seriously injured with anything as tragic as a head injury or a broken spine. She scoots her way down the embankment missing her footing a few times and scraping herself all over as she does.

Finally, she sees baby Don laying on what is the only grassy patch on the ground. Elizabeth bends over to pick him up. *Oh my Gosh, he's so heavy!* She wonders why she is having such a challenge picking him up. It isn't until after a couple of unsuccessful tries that she realizes that her right arm is badly broken. Coming to that realization, she scoops him up the best she can and holds him securely against her chest.

"Don, Don, I'm so sorry!" She coos the words over and over again, hoping that her soft voice will somehow act as a salve and heal the trauma he has just experienced.

While consoling her child, she recognizes that she is holding a living miracle in her arms. She gets the definite impression that her baby boy is special, even if she doesn't know exactly how or why.

"Jesus," Elizabeth exclaims aloud, "this baby must mean something to You. Thank You, Jesus! Thank You, Jesus!" She pours out her gratitude to God for saving her baby boy. It occurs to Elizabeth that an angel must have surely protected this baby because, against all natural laws on earth, Don is not only alive, but he doesn't have a scratch on him.

She makes her way back up the hill, praying with each uncertain step that she takes. Her ankles are unsteady, her legs are weak, her right arm is broken, and she is carrying a screaming child, yet she balances the best she can.

Soon, she approaches the wreck to see that a small crowd is gathered around the car. A man wearing a pair of murky green overalls runs over to her. A stout red-faced lady follows closely behind him.

"Honey, are you okay?" the lady inquires. She holds out her hand for Elizabeth to give her the baby but Elizabeth has a death-grip on the child. "It's okay sweetie," the lady reassures her, understanding the situation. "I'll hold him for you. He'll be just fine; just fine!" Elizabeth offers up Don and the lady cradles him gently.

"It's okay baby," the woman says softly. Don finally stops crying. It doesn't occur to Elizabeth that the way she was carrying the baby in her left arm while fighting her way back to the road was uncomfortable and at times even painful for him.

More people gather around Elizabeth. The man in the jumpsuit looks at Elizabeth. He gives her his warmest smile and offers, "Here Ma'am, let me help you." He gallantly picks her up and carries her over to his wagon. Elizabeth is grateful because her legs are just about to give out. The lady follows closely beside Elizabeth with little Don, now exhausted and asleep.

∞

The guardian who had carried little Don in his protective arms and laid him on the tuft of grass, is pleased that Elizabeth recognizes God's intervention on behalf of her son. He smiles to himself. He has fought a good fight today and has secured the child from the harm that was intended against him. This assignment has not been an easy one so far, and he knows that he has to be on the alert.

∞

In the end, Elizabeth's assessment of the situation is more correct than she had first thought. The baby is the only one to leave the accident unscathed. Sally was dragged some distance by the car and some of her ribs and her left collar bone are fractured. Worst of all, the left side of her face is partially scraped off.

Charlie was stuck under the car with gasoline pouring down on him. He was so terrified that he said his "last rites" confessional right then and there. It was then that the townsfolk who were gathered around learned that he is a married man with two little darling daughters at home in neighboring Parisburg.

Fortunately, the kind folks of Pulaski and the horse that he almost hit, worked together to lift Charlie's car in order to drag him out from underneath it. Unfortunately, Charlie's spine is crushed in two places. Neither Elizabeth nor Sally sees Charlie anymore, but Elizabeth will never forget that tragic day.

CHAPTER 3

ENCOUNTER WITH KATE

Elizabeth's dad owns a thousand acres of pure mountain with some of the hardest rocks in Blacksburg. From the top of the peak, on the creaky front porch of her father's clapboard house where Elizabeth sits, she smells sulfur intermittently assaulting the cool spring air. Looking down at the base of the mountain where the New River flows, she sees the Hercules Powder Plant that keeps most of the menfolk at Blacksburg employed.

Her father is one of the many miners who work at the coal mine a mile up from the powder plant. Even though her father prefers to be a farmer, he needs the 16 dollars per week that the plant provides. Elizabeth smiles as she listens to him digging up rocks so that he can make a patch of ground suitable enough to plant his beans, tomatoes, and corn.

Today, he is laboring without his trusty work-horse and companion, Kate. Kate is in the old barn spending precious time taking care of her newborn foal.

Like clockwork, the 3:00 p.m. train loaded down with coal on its way from the mine, lets out a long whistle, thereby telling Elizabeth that her resting spell is over.

"Goodness, it's getting late. I better start on dinner," she says. She thinks aloud about what she wants to prepare. "Cornbread! Eggs, milk, cornmeal." She gets up and wipes her hand across her forehead pushing back wispy strands of stray hair. She steps down off the porch and heads toward the barn to grind the corn.

∞

Don's eyes follow Elizabeth. He has woken up from his nap, and after looking for her, he finally sees her. At sixteen months old, he is proficiently putting one chubby little leg in front of the other and walking several feet without falling down. Despite the dirt and rocks underneath his bare little feet, he is steadily making progress as he follows after his mother. He gets halfway to the barn before his little legs give way and he begins to crawl.

In the barn, Elizabeth has pulled out several husks of dried corn and is pushing off the pebbly yellow kernels with her thumb when she becomes aware of her little one's presence. Unfortunately, Kate sees Don first. It is Kate's maddening snorts that cause Elizabeth to turn and look out of the barn door.

Elizabeth witnesses the horse raising herself up on her hind legs and neighing fiercely before coming down on Don. Elizabeth lets out a frightening scream and lunges through the crusty barn door. Kate, already up in the air to have a second go at Don, in response to Elizabeth's siren-like scream, twists her powerful body in midair towards the startling sound. When the horse comes down on all fours, she misses Elizabeth's baby by mere inches.

Elizabeth dives next to the horse.

"Oh God help me!" she prays as she lifts up her still baby. Kate smashed Don's arm to the point where his dangling limb is held onto his body by only skin.

Elizabeth runs to the house for help. She cries out to her father, "Dad! Oh Dad, Don's dead!!"

Her father stops skinning the groundhog that he shot earlier to go with Elizabeth's cornbread, and runs out to see his grandson, silent and limp in Elizabeth's arms. He realizes the gravity of the situation and knows that they need divine intervention. "Dear God, let him live. Don't let him suffer. Let this be as if it didn't happened. In Jesus' name, Amen."

After his quick prayer, he rushes to the barn and hitches Kate up to the wagon while Elizabeth bundles up Don in her wooly brown blanket. Her father comes back within minutes and she climbs up next to him.

The rickety dirt-crusted wagon rolls and dips as they travel along the long dirt road to Brother Snodgrass's house a mile up the way. Elizabeth keeps eyes on the fragile little boy. She feels grateful that her father takes her and the children into his home. She spends most of her time "in between jobs" on the farm; she never imagined any harm would come to them there.

Don's little arm looks like a broken hinge; his left shoulder and rib cage are swollen. Elizabeth is relieved to discover that he isn't dead; though she finds it strange that he hasn't cried once during this entire crisis.

Elizabeth prays the entire trip. "Thank you, God, that he is sleeping. Thank you, God, that he is not crying. Thank you, God, that Kate didn't crush him. Thank you, God, that he is okay. Thank you, God, for getting us to the doctor safely. Thank you, God, that you are gonna heal his arm."

Elizabeth is grateful that Brother Snodgrass is home. As they ride in his car to the hospital, she thanks God for good neighbors and for the help that she will receive at the hospital when she gets there.

Afterwards, on the way back home with a little child that looks mummified in cast and bandages, she prays.

"Thank you God for saving Don's life once again!"

Today is one day that Elizabeth will never forget. First, her little boy is alive and, second, she finds out that angels have command over horses.

Chapter 4

STOLEN CHILDHOOD

Seven-year old Don is mesmerized by the tall stranger. He doesn't know that he is the man who owns the shack he lives in and that his mom works for one of the man's rich relatives. He also doesn't know that this man is from one of the most influential political families in the state of Virginia.

Elizabeth is in the middle of addressing her employment situation. "Mr. Ray, I want to come and clean that house Sir, but I don't have anybody to take care of my son," she offers her excuse, hoping that he won't be too angry with her.

"Don't worry 'bout that. I'll take care of your son," Mr. Ray suggests. "I have to go downtown and run a few errands. The boy can come with me, if you don't mind."

"Mind!" Elizabeth gasps in surprise, "that would be great."

She bends down to spit-clean some smudge off of her little boy's face. "Don, you just be good now, y'hear. Do what Mr. Ray tells you like a good boy." She half-croons this statement at him but he still hears that warning tone in her voice.

"Thanks Mr. Ray. Just drop him off by the house. I'll be home around four."

Elizabeth feels good that Don will get to spend the day with a man like Mr. Ray. Tommy still isn't accepting of Don; he has been icy towards the boy ever since he returned from the navy. She didn't expect him to warm-up to the child overnight, but after four years, she thought that he would be more loving toward her boy. She plans on using Tommy's last name when she enrolls Don in school. She hopes that if the child was to be called Don Johnson, Tommy will feel better about her son.

"Have a good time, Don. I'll see you later today." Elizabeth hurriedly leaves her son in the hands of Mr. Ray.

∞

Don is thrilled! Finally, he is going to go downtown in a fancy car with this kind man. He never gets to spend time with his dad.

This is going to be great! he thinks as he excitedly climbs in the front seat. He doesn't know whether to look at all the shiny buttons and fancy gadgets or whether to look out the window and enjoy the scenery which seems particularly beautiful from behind the windows of this elegant car.

Mr. Ray turns towards Don and smiles as he drives. "You like this car, boy?" He senses that Don is captivated by this new situation.

"Ugh-huh" Don nods in confirmation. He isn't sure what to say to this stranger. He prefers not to talk to him at all. He wants to touch the shiny knobs.

The one-way conversation continues. "Listen," says Mr. Ray, "I gotta stop at one of my properties up a ways. I gotta pick up a couple a things. I won't be long. Okay."

Don nods some more.

Mr. Ray soon pulls up to a house that is planted in a yard dotted with yellow dandelions amid giant, knee-high rag-weeds. The weather-beaten house hasn't had company for years. Mr. Ray steps out of the car.

"Come on out, boy."

Don jumps out of the car and skips through the forest of weeds all the way to the steps of the big house.

Mr. Ray steps onto the porch and the worn wood underneath his feet creaks out a moan.

He looks back at Don. "Come on up, boy. The house ain't gonna bite ya."

Don bounds up the steps. He has never been in a house as big as this one before. He can tell that nobody lives in it. *How could anyone not live in such a big house?* he wonders. The shack he lives in can almost fit on the sizeable front porch.

Mr. Ray pushes the front door open. The door resists for a moment before responding to his touch.

"Come on in, son." Mr. Ray stands by the open door and motions for Don to go pass him.

The front room isn't as dark as Don imagined it to be. The broken window panes allow the bright sun to shine in. The heavy layer of dust all around gives the room a smoky eeriness.

"Come here, son."

Don turns his wide-eyed gaze from the big room to Mr. Ray.

"Come here!"

Don moves toward Mr. Ray and as he does, he hears the crack of broken glass under his feet. He looks down to see shards of a busted window pane scattered on the floor.

Mr. Ray doesn't wait for Don to move any closer, he takes two large steps towards the boy and tightly wraps one hand around Don's bony little arm.

He puts a little pressure on the boy's shoulders, forcing the child downward.

Crack! A broad piece of glass is made smaller when Don's knees buckle on top of it. What Mr. Ray does next is unspeakable; he proceeds to abuse the child in inexplicable ways.

∞

For Don, riding downtown in the fancy car is like riding in the back of a hearse. The shattered soul inside his trembling body is closed down. His eyes see nothing. No shiny buttons, no fancy gadgets, no trees along the side of the road, and no blue sky with puffy clouds overhead.

Distantly, his ears register that Mr. Ray is speaking to him.

"You say a word about what just happen here and your Mama will never work in this town again. Ya hear me!" Mr. Ray threatens in a gruff voice. "Even if you try to tell somebody, nobody will believe ya, you little hill-billy."

Mr. Ray's words brand themselves on Don's brain.

"Your family is trash, boy. Poor white trash! Nobody is going to believe your craziness over me!" Mr. Ray gives Don a despising look. Don's downcast eyes see his big toe pushed through his floppy shoes, and he sees the bruises on his bony knees. He knows that Mr. Ray is right.

"My family runs this town. People won't believe you over me."

The man keeps talking, "Your family will kick you out of your house and the people will kick you out of this town if you say a word that I did anything to ya. You won't even have a place to live."

Mr. Ray continues to talk, but Don is lost in a whirlwind of fear and terror. While the car rumbles into downtown, the boy's body continues to shake on its own accord, his stomach tightens and vomit threatens to rise up in his throat.

His thoughts are broken puzzle pieces jumbled haphazardly in his mind. His soul is splintered like the shards of broken glass scattered on the old floor where he was raped.

Though horrifying flashes of Don's experience assail his mind, one impression, though unseen, is just a real. Don knows that during that tragic violation, he also felt a supernatural presence enter his body. It crept in through some portal at the bottom of his feet, traveled up his legs, filled his whole body before it settled inside his head. Even now, foreign emotions rise up inside the little boy to the point where he feels like he will burst from it. Terror and helplessness grips him in an inescapable vice, and underneath that, a raging anger fights to release itself.

The inside of him swells with darkness and hopelessness. He knows that he has been killed and that he is powerless to take back his life.

His heart swells with a kind of fury that he has never known before. His only sound thought is, *I am going to kill you, kill you, kill you!* Mr. Ray keeps talking and Don knows that he is not able to kill Mr. Ray, so he closes his little eyes and wishes with all his might that he will disappear and that Mr. Ray cannot see invisible people.

∞

When they arrive downtown, Mr. Ray stops in front of the little country store that his family owns.

"Come on in, Don." That's the first time Mr. Ray uses his name. "Let's buy you some candy."

Candy no longer means something sweet to Don, and he has no desire for it, but he knows better than to not comply with Mr. Ray, so he obediently gets out of the car, surprised that he can stand upright on his rubbery legs.

∞

The front section of the store is a haven for children. It has colorful candies in glass jars which are lined up on the front counter. There are jawbreakers, squirrel nuts, hard candies of various flavors, bubble gum, and licorice.

"Hi Mabel! How are you this fine day?"

"Fine, Mr. Ray."

"Who you got there?" asks Mabel. From across the counter, the woman turns a smiling face towards the little boy by the doorway.

"That's Elizabeth's son. I'm watching him for a little while."

Mabel gives Don an extra special smile before turning her full attention to Mr. Ray. "That sure is nice of you, Mr. Ray," she says.

Mr. Ray smiles back and turns his attention to the candy jars. "Let me have twenty cents worth of a little bit of each in a poke bag. Mix it up, will ya."

∞

Later in the day, Mr. Ray drops Don off at his house. Except for his unusual silence, Elizabeth does not notice that her son has changed. Don hands Shelby the poke bag full of candy. His brother thinks that Santa Claus paid him a personal visit. His little sister Wanda is beside herself with glee. And, Elizabeth is tickled pink that charming Mr. Ray is such a thoughtful and caring man.

Don doesn't eat any of the candy.

"Don, what's wrong with you?" Shelby asks quizzically. Both his hands and his mouth are full of candy. "All this candy and you don't want none?" Shelby knows that something is strange, but he is lost in a world of hard candy and licorice. Shelby can never, in the innocence of his mind, imagine the truth.

Dead people don't eat candy. Don is a corpse; even if his breathing fools his family into thinking that he is alive.

∞

Outside, two demons hover above the roof of the tiny cabin. They take pleasure in the knowledge that they have had their fill of their own sweets today. Fat with pleasure and satiated with lust, they boast about the new host that they have acquired today. Proud of their great accomplishment, they take-off like twin bullets at lightning speed, anxious to give a full report of their successful day at work.

Chapter 5

THE AFTERMATH

Over the ensuing months, the spring of childhood joy, freedom, and trust within Don's soul evolves into a combustion chamber of rage. He doesn't want anyone to touch him, though he doesn't have to worry about his mother hugging him because she never does. Yesterday, he yelled at her. "Just leave me alone!" He resolved that she was the one who gave him over to Mr. Ray and did not come to save him. She also didn't come for him last year when that other man came to get him and he had run away.

Don thinks back to the fat man who had come to their cabin the previous year; he remembers what he had heard. "You know if he comes with me, he will have his own room," the man told him mom. "I have a lot of space at my house. My son here can use another little boy to play with." The man looks down at the chubby little child holding onto his coat jacket.

Don looks up at his mom, her arms folded across her chest; her lips pursed tightly together, her face expressionless. The man continued, "He'll be well cared for. Things are good; plus he'll fatten up in my family. Lord knows we isn't wanting for food." He pats his stout gut as if to make his point. The man continued talking but Don didn't hear much more.

"My mom is looking to give me away." he reasoned. He looked at his mom again; her face looked like a stone. "It's up to Don," she said dryly.

Don remembers the horrifying feeling that came over him when he had realized that at any second he would be grabbed and led away by this stranger. He'd shot off into the wooded mountains. Fear pursued him though he ran farther and farther away from the cabin. Finally, he'd stopped and hid behind a giant tree, hoping that neither the man nor his mom would find him. As the hours passed, and the daylight began to disappear, Don's heart sunk in despair. His mom did not come for him; he did not her hear call. It was Shelby's voice that he had heard calling his name as he sat shivering against that giant tree. It was Shelby who had come for him in the dark hours of the evening. It was Shelby who'd asked him to come home. When he finally walked through the front door, his mother did not even turn to look at him. Still unsure of his fate, he shot by her and went to hide under the blankets. Later, he heard everyone eating their supper, but his mother didn't call for him then either. He wouldn't have answered anyway; he couldn't risk being caught. Now, looking back, he accepts the sad truth, *"I know you don't love me, Mom."* *he concludes.*

Don doesn't play with Shelby and Wanda much and when he does, someone usually gets hurt. Sometimes he even hurts himself. Last week, while playing hide-and-seek, he whacked his head on the underside of the table. The spot still feels tender. A couple days ago, he elbowed Wanda in the jaw. She ran crying to their mother.

"Mom, Don hit me, again!"

His mom responded the same way she has been responding these days. "Don! What is wrong with you?" she had screamed at him.

Don hung his head down, in hopes that she would think that he was sorry, but he wasn't.

Elizabeth had ordered him to go out and get her a good switch off of the tree out back. "I'm gonna beat your little hiney!" She made good on her promise.

He doesn't like getting beat with the switch, and as far as his memory serves him, he didn't use to get beat this much before that thing happened to him. *When I get big, I'm gonna beat everybody with a huge giant switch.*

He hates being different; he is angry about how different he is. He is angry that he is scared of most everything these days. He is scared that someone will find out about Mr. Ray and that his family will be kicked out of their home because of him.

Don also doesn't sleep as well. Sometimes he has bad dreams of monsters coming to get him. Other times, he senses them lying down beside him. Before he goes to bed each night he says the prayer that his mom taught him.

> *Now I lay me down to sleep.*
> *I pray the Lord my soul to keep.*
> *And if I die before I wake,*
> *I pray the Lord my soul to take.*

Sometimes it keeps the monsters away, but sometimes the prayer doesn't work.

The biggest problem he has right now is that he wets the bed. With everyone sleeping together in the same bed, peeing in bed will be particularly unpleasant when it gets cold. Buried under the weight of multiple layers of blankets, in temperature so cold that the dishwater turns to ice, will only creates more of a problem. He prays, *Oh God, please let me stopping peeing in the bed.*

Don gets angry with himself for doing these bad things. On the outside, he still looks the same and he wonders how that could be, since he knows on the inside that he is different. He tries to not act any differently because he doesn't want his family to be kicked out onto the street because of him.

Most times, Don wishes that he was invisible. That way, he could hide when he gets in trouble and his mom would never find him. Being invisible is a superpower that he could use to hide from monsters, especially monsters like that Mr. Ray. He also senses that somebody he cannot see is watching him. Perhaps it's another monster.

He thinks, *When I get my superpowers, I'm gonna kill you!*

Chapter 6

THE VISITOR

Elizabeth, Tommy, Don and his siblings are moving to another house. Tommy has made an arrangement with the owner where he will fix up the gentleman's house in exchange for rent, which is not only affordable, but downright cheap. This new house is like nothing they have lived in so far. It has six rooms! Two are bedrooms, and one is a living room. It also has a small kitchen and a bathroom complete with indoor plumbing and a working toilet. In the living room are two large windows that face the front yard.

Elizabeth admires the curtains that she's made from a floral material that was once a bed sheet belonging to one of her clients. She pinches herself at being so lucky to get this place. It is ideal. Now Elizabeth can take a break from going up to her father's place so often.

The squeak of the opening front door breaks her musing.

"Hey!" Tommy greets her. He bounces in the house carrying a small bag with fatback. He cashed his paycheck and didn't drink it all this time. Today is what the kids call "a good-eating day".

"Where are the boys?" Elizabeth asks.

"They're bringing in the rest of the groceries." Tommy replies.

Elizabeth walks passed him, and almost bumps into Shelby as he comes up the two steps leading into the house.

"Hey Mom," Shelby greets her.

"Hi, where's Don?"

"He's coming," Shelby replies as he heads to the kitchen counter.

Walking out, Elizabeth is met by a petrified little eight-year old.

Don cannot believe what has just happened to him. Turning from picking up the peanut butter out of the trunk of the car, he sees the ugliest creature imaginable standing behind one of the living room windows. Its large bulging eyes held him prisoner in a hypnotic stare. Frozen in place, he could do nothing else but stare back at the scaly brown giant that showed its fangs as it laughed at him.

When his mom walked out of the door, the demon turned its head away; only then was Don able to move.

Don trembles as Elizabeth reaches for him; he begins to come to his wits while his mom holds his hand.

"Doh...doh...don't go in the house!" he stammers out wildly.

"Don't go back in the house, Mom. The devil is in there. Don't let him get us, Mom."

Suddenly, he lets go and frantically runs inside the house. *I must save my family!*

Running into the house, he cries, "Don't go into that room!"

Tommy and Elizabeth decide to help dispel their son's fear by walking into the living room and then going from room to room to show him that there are no monsters in the house.

"See, Don, nobody is here," assures Elizabeth. Shelby makes a grand gesture by looking under the table and under the beds. Wanda follows everyone else and looks behind the bedroom door. Elizabeth puts her hand on Don's head to console him, "It's okay, baby. There's nothing here to be afraid of."

Elizabeth, however, believes her son's every word. She saw him when his skin was white with fear and she recognizes that he is truly panicked. In fact, Elizabeth, like many other people in her family, acknowledges that there is more to this world than meets the eye.

Suddenly, she remembers something and turns to Tommy. "Hey, wasn't Bud's coffin laid out right underneath this same window?" She remembers that a week before, her deceased brother was displayed in that exact spot. *That man was a real Christian man. I don't know what the devil is going on here.*

She wonders what the presence of this unwelcome visitor means, and why it is her little Don that saw what remains unseen to most people. "Lord, help this child," she prays. She has no doubt that what her little boy saw is real.

Chapter 7

A BRAVE MOVE

If Elizabeth has a favorite place in Pulaski, it is the post office. The post office is her connection to the outside world. She most always goes to the post office with a sense of hope and adventure. Her brother Eugene loves writing as much as she loves getting his letters. Lately, he has been encouraging her to move to the promise-land of Baltimore.

His letters fill her head with the hope that she will never again have to track down houses to clean because Baltimore is full of people with houses that are *waiting* for someone like her to clean them.

I'm telling you, Elizabeth, just the other day one lady at work asked if I knowd anybody that could help her out. That's one more job you missed out on Lizzy, Eugene writes.

Elizabeth's heart sinks a little as she reads this. *Yeah, I did miss that boat. I can really use the money too.*

Eugene's words are simply animated with excitement. *We got row houses here Liz. There are like twenty houses on one block! Twenty, Liz!* He emphasizes his point so that she can get a better idea of the vast amount of houses and the insurmountable amount of clients that she can potentially have in Baltimore.

In this recent letter, Elizabeth hears Eugene's words as if he was standing right in front of her.

You just got to open your mouth and, BAM! You got a job!

Elizabeth reads all of Eugene's letters about her bright future in the big city and finally she is convinced that she can do more for herself and her children if she moves to Baltimore. In the four years since her youngest, Pat, was born, Tommy has hardly been any help. She is motivated to seek out greener and more lucrative pastures.

She ponders Eugene's promise from his last letter; *You and the kids can stay with us until you get a place. We got lots of room Lizzy.*

Elizabeth feels a surge of hope. The year 1954 is the year of Elizabeth Lucado Johnson. She has never heard of one person leaving the mountains of Pulaski to go and live outside of these hills. And, she definitely has never heard of anyone from her small town going to live in the big city of Baltimore.

"If Eugene can leave Blacksburg, I sure as heck can leave Pulaski," she says aloud to herself. With this, the deal was sealed.

∞

Spring is here. Robins and cardinals are looking to make their new nests, and so is Elizabeth. She boards the Greyhound bus for Baltimore with her old suitcase and four burlap bags; just enough for her and her children to carry. Finally arriving, Elizabeth carefully matches the letters on the piece of paper with the sign that reads *Eutaw Street*. It is a relief to finally arrive at Eugene's door: 1300 Eutaw St.

Tling! Tling! She presses the doorbell by the building's entrance.

Tling! Tling!

She waits a breath or two then presses it again, anxious to set herself and her load down for a much deserved rest.

Tling. Tling. Tling

Five minutes pass. Elizabeth surmises that no one is home but she continues to touch the doorbell because she has nothing else to do and nowhere else to go. The kids pull at her skirt as they complain of being tired.

Tling. Tling. Tling. Tling. Tling.

"Mr. Lucado moved," a voice behind her announces. Elizabeth turns to see an elderly lady holding a little fluffy poodle in her arms. The miniature mutt has its long tongue hanging out its panting mouth. The dog twists its head back and forth attempting to lick the veined fingers grasping him.

"He moved out two days ago," the lady volunteers before asking, "You kin?"

"He moved?" Elizabeth repeats in disbelief. This doesn't make sense.

Elizabeth checks the house numbers nailed into the brownish-red bricks of the building with the numbers on the piece of paper in her hand.

"No, he didn't move Ma'am," Elizabeth corrects the lady. "He just went somewhere. He'll be back." She tries to assure herself.

"No," the lady retorts, "his whole family packed up a truck and moved out a couple-a-days ago."

The lady narrows her eyes and squints suspiciously at Elizabeth and her brood. "I live next door," she declares as if to say that there is no point in arguing the facts that she has just stated.

"Who are *you*?" the woman asks Elizabeth pointedly. Elizabeth introduces herself and tells the lady her story.

"I'm sorry hon, but I don't know what to tell you. He's gone and he didn't tell me where he was going." The woman fishes her keys out of her purse. "I hope you find him," she says as she and her dog go inside leaving Elizabeth and her brood on the verge of tears.

Elizabeth and her children spend the next eight hours sitting on the benches in the park across the street. Though she tries to hold back her tears for the sake of the children; few still spill over. It is getting dark and she doesn't want to move away from the only spot in Baltimore that she knows.

Oh God, we will have to sleep in the park tonight. She resigns herself to this distinct possibility. She decides on two fairly clean benches underneath a redwood tree a few feet away from the sidewalk.

The children are consistently complaining and fussing mostly because they are hungry. She hopes that they do not sense the magnitude of her desperation.

"We are waiting for Uncle Eugene to come for us," she reassures them. "Just be patient. Don't worry, he'll be here soon." She says these words to dispel her own fears as well.

She gives each child a swallow of the last of the sugar water from the mason jar. Her last three dollars is not enough money to go back to Pulaski, and she doesn't know where to go for help.

"Oh God, please help me!" she prays. She knows no one else can help her in this situation. She leans back, too emotionally and physically exhausted to hope. She knows that God sees her desperation.

At 6:30 p.m., Elizabeth catches the moment when the street lights of the city switch on. She then looks across the street and watches as a truck pulls up in front of 1300 Eutaw Street. To her amazement, her brother steps out.

Later, she finds out that Eugene had only stopped by on his way home from work to pick up a small table which he had forgotten!

∞

Nine-year-old Don remembers the day when his family moved in with Uncle Eugene. It was a very miserable day. He was suffering with a sore throat and he begged his mother for something to drink but all he got was sweet sugar-water. He didn't mind, but his throat wanted more than just a sip. He didn't know that at the time that he was developing a bad case of tonsillitis.

It is a blustery day that invites brisk walking but Don and his sister are idly inching their way several blocks down the street to The Ear, Nose, and Throat Hospital. Don is scheduled for surgery today. His mother has to work so Wanda is accompanying him to the hospital.

They arrive at the front desk looking red-faced and wind-burned.

"Where's your mom?" the admitting nurse inquires.

"She's at work." Wanda replies. "She'll come by when she gets off."

Sufficiently satisfied with that reply, the nurse asks a couple more questions and then admits Don.

Wanda walks back home leaving her brother in the capable hands of the hospital staff.

The friendly nurses promise him ice cream after his surgery and within an hour, a much less reluctant Don is laying on the operating table.

One of the nurses, whom he particularly likes, looks down at him. "Okay, son, I'm going to put this mask over your face. You take a nice breath and you start counting backwards from one hundred; alright." She smiles and says again, "You know how to do that, don't you?"

The nurse puts the cup of anesthetic gas over Don's face for him to breathe in. From his first breath, Don immediately feels like he is spinning around in a circle. The circle keeps getting smaller and smaller and when he gets to the center of it, he hears a clear and distinct voice. He knows that it is not the voice of either the doctor or the two nurses in the room.

You're crazy. You're crazy. You're crazy. The voice says over and over again.

After a while it announces a new message, *You are going to die. YOU are going to DIE!*

Finally, it follows up with a horrible, mimicking laugh. *HA! HA! HA! HA!* Fear coils around Don and he is helplessly trapped in its grasp.

∞

"We will take care of him once and for all!" says one demonic minion who has successfully robbed many souls on operating tables. "This will not be a problem," he says confidently. He turns and begins to tell his cohorts that he witnessed an attack that was successful in diverting the attention of the menacing angel who was constantly by Don's side.

∞

After work, Elizabeth hurriedly walks into the hospital.

"Oh God, be with this child, I pray." She has a strong urge to pray for her son. She prays, yet the urgent feelings persist. "Thank you Jesus for guiding the surgery. Thank you, Jesus, for holding the doctor's hand. Thank you, Jesus, for being with Don."

Elizabeth's pace quickens as she reaches the hospital. A quick stop at the front desk gives her directions to Don's room. She walks in with the intention of greeting her groggy son with a lollipop and a big smile, but from the moment that her eyes land on his face, she immediately knows that something is wrong.

Don's pale face looks drained of blood and she can tell that he is not breathing.

"Nurse!" Elizabeth screams aloud. Her call gets the attention of the staff. A doctor in the next room rushes in. Two nurses quickly follow. Elizabeth watches helplessly as they swing the heavy iron bed away from the cramped corner, pull aside the bed sheets and begin to resuscitate her boy.

Their quick actions save Don's life.

Elizabeth knows that God has answered her prayers once again. She reflects on all the near tragic incidents that have happened to this child. More has happened to him than to all her other children combined. She looks up to Heaven and chides herself. "Oh God, I have to pray more."

∞

The angel, with renewed strength, fights his way through the barricade of demons that gang upon him. He has a charge and he will not fail to keep it. He arrives in time, strengthened and empowered, to abort a ghastly assignment.

∞

Don knows that his life is in danger. Others might attribute his near-death experience to the surgery, but he knows the moment when the invisible person put its hand over his face. This is not the first time that a demon tried to suffocate him.

Chapter 8

TAKING CARE OF BUSINESS

"Shelby, hurry up, I'm freezing!" Don feels the cold from the bottom of his feet all the way into his deepest insides. He shakes as he looks behind him to see the toe prints that he has left in the snow.

"Come on Shelby, let's go!"

"It's not my fault you're cold. Why didn't you put the cardboard inside your shoes?"

Don furrows his brow in annoyance. He needs a pair of shoes that has soles on them. He feels pain in his right leg every time he puts weight on his foot. His toes are frost bitten but he has to keep walking.

"Shelby, if you want to lollygag around, then go ahead. I'm gone." Don leaves Shelby dragging a piece of wood in the snow. Don longs for summer to come. At least, in the summer the only things he has to be careful of stepping on are lit cigarette butts.

As soon as they enter the house, their mother greets them with an unexpected monologue. "Guys, I need to talk to you. You know that Tommy and I don't always get along and that I have good reason to come here without him..."

She pauses as if looking to find the right words. Not having much luck, she decides to get to the point. "Well, he is coming up in the spring to live with us."

"Great!" Shelby exclaims.

"Big deal!" Don mutters. Whether Tommy lives with them or not doesn't make much difference to him.

Elizabeth gives her thirteen-year-old a disparaging look, "Mind your attitude!" she retorts.

Don backs down but thinks to himself, *It isn't like he ever stays around us long anyway. I ain't blind. He got another family somewhere, and you know it too!*

An hour later, Don looks at his feet wrapped up in toasted newspaper and thinks about Tommy coming down to live with them. He figures that Tommy's arrival will mean extra money coming into the house and that might mean a new pair of shoes. *I guess Tommy's okay*, Don resolves to himself.

∞

Spring brings both warm weather and Tommy's arrival from Pulaski. Tommy gets a job as a carpenter almost immediately. Six days into working and he is already due a paycheck. The household is elated with anticipation of this much needed income.

"I'm gonna take you guys out to the movies tonight," Tommy tells Shelby and Donnie at the breakfast table. "This evening when I come home, you all be ready. Okay."

"Oh yeah, we'll be ready." The boys look at each other and smile broadly. Don thinks about the other boys in his neighborhood who have fathers that give them money for movies, but he and Shelby usually have to find soda pop bottles to sell to the local store up the street. At a penny a bottle, they'd hustle to get enough for a movie.

More often, however, by the time they get their twenty cents together, their friends would be leaving the theatre.

Don zealously digs into the pancakes that Elizabeth prepares from flour and water. He pours more of the syrup that she makes by mixing sugar and water into a syrupy elixir.

Thank goodness Tommy is here, Don thinks as he eats his mom's flour pancakes. *Dad's gonna buy some real food for us.*

Don turns to Shelby who's licking the sugar water off of his plate. "You think Tommy will have enough money to buy us some bologna?" he asks.

Shelby's face lights up. "Bologna! We ain't had bologna since last Thanksgiving!"

"You know what, I'm gonna order me a big bag of popcorn tonight. We ain't ever had popcorn."

"I'm gonna buy me jawbreakers!"

This upcoming outing inspires celebration. "Let's go to the park and play some marbles till I make you look bad." jokes Shelby.

Don jumps up from the table, leaving the chair teeter-tottering to find its balance.

"You can try, but you know I always whup you."

Don says this, but he knows that he is all thumbs when it comes to flicking marbles. He will never forget the day, local reporters, hard up for a story, pulled up to the little park where he and Shelby were playing. They declared him a champion marble player and featured him in a filler story. The boys still make this their own private joke.

Don dashes from the kitchen and Shelby follows suit. Both boys race out the front door with marbles and ball in tow.

"Mom, we're across the street!" Don yells as they slam the door behind them.

Shortly afterwards, Elizabeth steps outside onto the small stoop of their apartment with her broom in hand, watching the boys while she sweeps.

A police car pulls up and stops in front of the apartment. Two policemen emerge and walk directly over to her.

"Mrs. Johnson?"

"Yeah."

"Ma'am, I'm sorry to say that I have some bad news for you." One takes off his smart blue hat and puts it to his chest.

"Your husband, Mr. Thomas Johnson, had a fatal heart attack around nine-thirty this morning." He looks down at the piece of paper he had written the information on, to make sure that he'd gotten the name correctly.

Elizabeth lets out a wail. As if on the same cue, both boys immediately look over at the house to see the police officers talking in their mom.

Dashing across the street, the policemen greet the children with a weary smile. They do not appear to be in a hurry to leave.

Looking at Don standing closer in proximity, one says, "Son, we are so sorry about your father."

The officers stay for another ten minutes and proceed to tell the boys and their mother that Tommy was on top of a scaffold, fixing a window, when he had a heart attack. He fell off the scaffold and died.

In the night, all five of them escape from the confines of their home. Elizabeth takes Shelby, Don, Wanda, and little Pat for a walk down to the Harbor, a half-block from the city morgue. She chooses a bench with a grassy spot around it to sleep on. They prefer to spend the hot summer night in the company of the drunks sprawled on the sidewalk by the rancid waterfront, than to stay in the apartment without Tommy.

The pancakes are the only meal that the children ate. The boys know there will be no bologna, there will be no movies, and there will be no help for their mother.

The next morning, Elizabeth takes the girls back home while Don and Shelby stay behind to fish green bananas out of the dirty harbor. Bananas sometimes fall out of the crates when they are being unloaded off the ships. The boys don't care that they have to push aside rusty cans, sewage, old newspapers, broken crates, or drowned rats, in order to get these bananas. They are just grateful that they don't encounter a carcass of the occasional drunk that sometimes fall off the pier. Their broken hearts cannot take another death today.

Fishing for bananas helps Don to keep his feelings at bay. Sorrow, anger, and disbelief all force their way upon Don's mind and he struggles to keep the tears from spilling over. As he walks along the edge of the harbor, his thinks about his family. Right now, his family needs these bananas for dinner tonight and there is nobody else to help his mom, just him and Shelby. He comes to the realization that if he is ever going to have anything in life, he will have to work for it himself. Tommy was hardly there to help out, and when he did come and say that he would help, he suddenly died.

Yes, Sir, Don tells himself, *whatever I gotta do, I gotta do!*

With this resolve, thirteen-year-old Don makes up his mind to become a business man of the streets of Baltimore.

∞

Don creates different means for making money. He sells newspapers, though more often than not, they are a day old. He goes into the neighborhood bars where the lights are too dim for people to see the date, and where the guys are too drunk to notice. By the time they realize it, Don already has their money.

He also sells flowers. Sometimes he rescues old flowers from the garbage cans behind Lexington Market, and other times, he buys leftovers from the florist there. On occasions, he even uses toilet paper to make flowers.

He often walks around with a shoe box like it is his business briefcase. Inside, he sometimes has individually wrapped gum sticks that he sells after breaking apart a pack.

People are willing to buy these things from a boy who looks like an orphan solely by the sad condition of his appearance.

Don meets up with Shelby at Fayette and Charles streets and they share the day's adventures with each other. Today, Don is particularly excited.

"Hey, Shelby, guess what? You know the yard we cut through behind our place?"

"Yeah."

"Well, this morning I found a real live baby bird. It must have fallen out of a tree or something."

"Where is it?" Shelby asks excitedly.

"I put it in my box and went down to Kelly's. One of them guys bought it from me. I was going out the door when I heard him telling his buddy that he was gonna go in the woods and free my little bird. Can you believe it? He was gonna just throw away a perfectly good bird!"

"No way. What'd you do?"

"Whad-you-mean, I snuck right back in there and stole the bird. That's good money he was getting rid of. Then I took it down to Joe's Bar and sold it again to some sap. Wanna see how much I made?"

"Sure. I can't believe it. That was real lucky, Don."

Don smiles and shows off the reward of his day's labor.

Shelby and Don switch stories of their adventures of being working men. Don always has better stories to tell, especially when he works as a shoe-shine pimp.

As a shoe-shine pimp, Don carries shoe polish and rags in his shoe-box and walks up and down the pier looking for customers. Right now, he's glad to see the sailors from the ship that's docked in the harbor.

"Shoe shine, Mister? Shoe shine?"

He begins his sales pitch with one eager-looking sailor.

"They have any women on your ship?" Don asks as he fervently spits-shine the shoes.

"No, man. I ain't had a woman in months!" the sailor replies.

"I know a *lot* of pretty girls," Don says. "Wanna meet one of 'em? An quarter extra for this shine and I'll introduce you to my friend Stacy."

Don gets his extra quarter after he takes the soldier to Stacy's apartment around the corner.

Once at Stacy's, Don receives a cut of Stacy's fee for his referral. That's another twenty five cents.

"Can you stay around a minute and watch my kid?" Stacy asks. She knows Don will babysit because they have an arrangement.

"Sure," Don replies.

He is happy to stay for twenty minutes while Stacy takes care of business in the next room. This babysitting is another job that means an additional fifteen cents in his pocket.

In the privacy of the small bathroom in Stacy's apartment, Don takes his money out and counts it.

He now has enough to give to his mom for groceries but he will not tell her where most of his money comes from.

"God, will you please bring me some more customers? We have to pay the light bill by Friday," Don prays.

He puts his money back, feeling proud that things are going well.

He muses; *I can't wait to tell Shelby about my day!*

∞

Everybody has their own business to take care of. Even those in the world of the invisible are busy.

Seven demons meet together to engage in discussion regarding Don's future. The atmosphere is sinister and froth with argumentativeness and discord. Each wanting to have his ideas chosen above the other, but one stands out among the rest.

"How about taking him down with alcohol?" one with rodent-like feature suggests.

"That is a powerful elixir. Subtle as first yet gets 'em in the end." agrees another.

This idea was one which each concede was ideal and could be carried out without much problem.

They bark and squabble over who will get the role of taking care of this task, but it is the one with the scaly skin that snatches the assignment away from the others.

Chapter 9

————— ·•■·• —————

NEW INTRODUCTIONS

Shelby raises his mug of Budweiser and hollers out, "HAPPY BIRTHDAY TO MY LITTLE BROTHER!"

Some men at the next table raise their drinks and smile at Don.

Shelby turns his attention to Don, "Don, you're twenty-one now; drink your beer."

Don decides that he will finish his first full mug of beer.

Encouraging himself to drink every drop, he chides himself, *You're a man now, Don, drink the stupid beer.*

Don has taken sips of other people's beer before and he hates the taste. Buying his own now doesn't make the beer taste any better.

Don feels glad that he has Shelby because for the most part, he is a loner. He talks when he has business to conduct, but he is not one to voluntarily hold a personal conversation with anyone. Few people can say that they truly know him; he's cantankerous most of the time which encourages folks to stay away. Don has no desire to know anyone on any personal level either.

"Here's to you, Shelby." Don says as he finishes the bitter pleasantness.

Don looks at Shelby from over the rim of his mug. He feels empty inside and void of love. He thinks to himself, *I don't know what you're doing here with me, Shelby.* Don doesn't feel close to anyone nor does he love anyone. His mind goes to his mother, his sisters, and other relatives, yet he feels nothing special for them, most particularly, his mother. His mind takes him down a path he doesn't want to entertain, especially on his birthday when he feels like his existence is a bone in his mother's craw. *You won't even tell me who my father is! Anyway, it's not like he wants me either.*

Shelby interrupts his thoughts, "Don, you're due. When are you gonna get a *real* girlfriend?"

"A *real* girlfriend." Don laughs at Shelby's wording.

"Yeah, it's time to give up 'dem hussies you hang around with." Shelby says it like a joke but he is also partly serious.

"A girlfriend? I'm not looking for one. Let's get another beer."

Inside his heart, Don doesn't think he is capable of falling in love with *anyone*. He doesn't want a steady girlfriend and he certainly isn't looking for one.

"Whoever this real girlfriend is, she better stay outta my way." Don and Shelby both laugh at his warning to this unknown female.

∞

Deciding to leave Florida with her friends and come to Baltimore "just because" isn't one of Ruth Moore's brighter decisions. Now, they tell her that they are going to crash over at some guy's house.

Don offers his place to Ruth, along with the other four "tenants" for a few days. He often has people stay in his apartment because he needs the extra money to help pay the bills. Also, he fears being by himself. Having people around makes him feel safe, even if he doesn't socialize with them.

This rainy Sunday afternoon marks Ruth's final day as a guest at Don's apartment. The shadow which the dark clouds cast over the sky along with the music of the rain on the zinc awning, provide a romantic atmosphere in the small living room. Don and Ruth talk quietly until the lazy lull inside the apartment cast a romantic spell on both of them. Don is all too happy at this unexpected twist of fate. Ruth leaves early the next morning after spending an unplanned evening with Don.

As the sun peers through the glass blocks in the bathroom window, Don stands over the commode feeling more and more relieved. He smiles to himself. *This was a great one-night stand!*

He is grateful to have someone close to him. He's spent too many nights alone. He feels boosted and energized.

This is great. I hope she catches her bus back to Florida in time, he thinks, satisfied that he will never have to see her again.

∞

The sun's been set for half an hour before Don drags his tired body home. He is looking forward to a long shower and catching up on the sleep that he sacrificed last night. Arriving at his building, he sees someone who he never expected to see again in his life. It's pretty Ruth Moore standing with her suitcase in her hands!

At nineteen, Ruth is not a girl to sleep around. She didn't intend to sleep with Don, but he was so sweet last night. And, when he touched her, she felt that he was the one that she was meant to be with. She didn't go searching for a boyfriend, but she is okay with the one that she found. She didn't think that love would ever find her, but now that it has, she is not about to let it go. She is also thankful because love couldn't have come at a more convenient time. Her residential situation in Florida is tentative at best.

"Hey handsome! I missed you." She says as she sashays over to Don and hugs him tightly. Don doesn't know what to say. He decides to use his lips to kiss her instead.

In the night, with Ruth lying beside him, Don thinks about the benefits he will gain by having a live-in girlfriend. One, he will have some constant companionship, and two, she will hear his alarm clock and then wake him up in the mornings so that he won't be late for work anymore.

∞

Don and Shelby recently joined the Local #1 Painter's Union where they mostly paint structures that are made of steel. Last week, they painted a water tank in

Dundalk, and this week they are assigned to paint a portion of the Bay Bridge.

Don sits silently in Shelby's car as they drive home from the job. He feels like he is going to burst. He was not ready for any added responsibility but after one year with Ruth, he is now a husband with a baby on the way. Home is the last place he feels like going right now.

"Hey, Shelby, let's stop and get a beer, huh?"

"Sure. What's up with you, anyway? You've been moping all day."

"It's Ruth, man."

"Ruth?"

"Yeah!" Don begins to share his feelings with Shelby. "I hardly know her, man."

Shelby bops his head up and down as he drives, encouraging Donnie to keep talking.

"I mean, what do I know about her? Now we got this baby coming and I have to work harder to provide for her and now this kid."

Shelby interjects, "Hey, a man's got to do what a man's got to do."

Don agrees. "Yeah! But I hate being in that house. All Ruth and I do is fight. I try talking to her but every time we end up arguing."

Don confesses his true feelings to Shelby, "Man, I don't love her. I tried, man. I really tried. I don't know nothing about loving somebody."

Shelby seems unphased by this confession. "Don, I thought you and Ruth were friends?"

Don is a little taken back.

"Friends? Shelby, I ain't got no friends."

Shelby is not keen on continuing the conversation about Don's marriage problems so he switches the focus of the conversation.

"No friends? Man, I got a ton! You need to loosen up Don and meet some people. You sit and don't talk to nobody. How do you expect to make friends?"

Donnie gives Shelby's words serious consideration. *It's true. Shelby has a lot of friends. I need to make me some friends so I don't have to go home all the time.*

Don takes a mental walk and looks over his social life. Most times, when he and Shelby come home from work they stop at Cheap Charlie's. Shelby, a veteran drinker, has a lot of friends; he is usually the life of the party there. Don sees himself sitting in Shelby's shadow nursing his one beer. He wants more. He wants friends, and if drinking like Shelby is a way to have friends, he is ready to take on a few beers.

At the bar, Don takes note of Shelby. He looks at Shelby laughing and he feels jealousy rising inside him. Shelby seems happy and he wishes that he could be like that. *God, why can't I laugh like that? You let things happen to me that don't happen to anybody else. You are not a fair God.*

He takes a few sips of his beer. Looking around, he sees one couple against the wall near the neon 'EXIT' sign, kissing like they're mining for gold. He feels his body react and thinks of Ruth. Anger replaces all stirring of desire.

That woman gives me nothing but a hard time. God, I can't even have peace inside my own house. What are you doing to me? I'm not going home tonight, I tell you that much. He picks up his drink and takes two big gulps.

The hubbub of conversation surrounds him but it makes him feel even more alone. He downs the rest of his beer, catches the eyes of the bartender, and motions for more by pushing his glass forward for another refill. Don feels increasingly angry about his life. His mind wonders about last night and many nights before that. A demon came into the bed and pinned him down by throwing its leg over him. Don closes his eyes tightly and grimaces his face in anger. He's sick of having to fight off demons, even in his sleep.

Don't I deserve some peace, God? How comes You allow this to happen to me in the first place? Why don't You help me? You are the One who is causing this to happen to me. I hate this stinking life. Don finishes his beer before getting up and leaving Shelby behind. He heads home even though he doesn't want to.

Chapter 10

WON OVER BY ALCOHOL

Within a couple years of his decision to start drinking, Don can truly say that he has friends. He is a regular at Cheap Charlie's, and he also knows some people at Last Call, and at Frederick's. Drinking loosens him up. He now has a lot of friends, especially when he is the one buying the drinks.

"Hey!" Don hollers out above the noise of the bar one day.

One or two people look at him strangely, but go back to their drinks.

"HEY!" He shouts louder.

The chatter dies down and curious faces turn in his direction.

Satisfied that his friends are paying attention, Don proudly announces, "I'm happy to say that my baby boy was born today!"

"Yeah!" a couple people cheer.

Most don't much care, but Don doesn't notice. He feels awesome. If he were a peacock, he would spread all his feathers and strut proudly across the floor.

"I wanna buy *everybody* a shot a whiskey. Let's drink to my baby boy, Billy!"

The bar erupts in applause. Don does not question whether the spontaneous cheer is on account of the free whiskey or whether it is for Billy. He feels like he has just scored the winning touchdown and his friends are bolstering him on their shoulders.

He struts around the floor and as he passes by the tables and by the stools at the counter; a number of people say congratulations. A few pat him on the back as acknowledgement. Two or three raise their shot glasses in his direction.

He thinks back to the conversation he had with Shelby a while earlier. He remembers that before, he couldn't stand the taste of alcohol, now it is something he loves. He has more friends, and being here, helps him to deal with the mess that is his life.

Back at his favorite stool, he raises his shot glass to his lips. He is thankful that he chooses to spend his hard-earned money to pay for drinks. *I deserve a little happiness in my life. God, you ain't using me like You said. So I'm gonna enjoy my life.*

He does not tell the people at the bar that his baby boy was born almost one thousand miles away from him. He doesn't tell them that Ruth and Melissa, his first born, moved back to Florida a month before their baby was born. And, he doesn't tell his friends that his relationship with whiskey and beer are partly responsible for Ruth's decision.

Looking down into the small glass of amber-colored liquid, he thinks back to when Ruth decided to leave him. It was a Friday; he had gotten his pay check and Ruth asked him to go to the store to buy a garbage can and a gallon of milk.

"Okay." he had said. He left but he did not return home. In fact, he came home two days later with no garbage can, no milk, and no money. He had spent his paycheck on women, playing pool, and on drinking. For two days, he drank and hung around his new friends. While he was drinking, Ruth left Baltimore with Billy in her belly and Melisa in her arms.

Painful thoughts!

"Bartender, give me another shot, will ya."

∞

Alcohol is not a kind friend to Don. It hasn't helped him in his family life and it doesn't help him on his job either.

At work, Don falls down while painting a steel tank at the Peach Bottom Power Plant in Pennsylvania. Standing atop the ten foot tank, his foot slips on the lid of the tank. Without the lid securely fastened, he falls into the tank, hitting the steel handrail on his way down.

Now, he has a nasty wound above him right eye. The gash is so deep that his flesh peels back and droops over his eye-socket and onto his cheek bone.

Shelby offers to take Don to the hospital but on the way there, they stop off for a quick drink.

Twelve hours later, they arrive at the hospital.

The emergency room nurse looks up at the clock. It's 2:00 a.m. and this smelly drunk is slouched on the chair across from her as she fills out his paperwork.

"How long ago did you get this cut?" the nurse asks.

"A couple hours ago," Don slurs.

The blood is fully coagulated and the skin is already grafted on to his cheekbone.

Several minutes later, an old doctor comes and looks at the mess that is Don's face.

"Sew him up," he orders. "These drunks mess themselves up and expect us to fix them." His lack of compassion is apparent.

A young intern is assigned to Don. The attention that he gives Don cannot be called *care* by any stretch of the imagination. He jabs the needle inside the nasty wound and pushes in some anesthetic. He thinks that the amount of alcohol in Don is enough to numb the pain that he is about to inflict. He scrubs off the wounded area without much tenderness, then rips the skin off Don's cheek bone and pulls it back up over his eye. Afterward, he sews it in place along Don's brow-line like he was suturing a turkey.

The severity of the pain sobers Don. He realizes that he had driven from Pennsylvania to get to this hospital in Baltimore and that he has no recollection of the trip because he was too drunk.

After being discharged, he drives home from the hospital with his head feeling like the doctor had bashed it in rather than sew it up. The thought occurs to him that his relationship with alcohol is not a good one.

"I swear I'll never drink again. Period! And, that is the last time I'll ever go to *that* God-forsaken hospital again."

Chapter 11

THE FINGER

Sparrows Point is a town that is very good to Don. His job at the steel mill is one of the best things that he has going for him. His hands are steady right now because earlier, he had time to drink down a couple of beers for breakfast.

"Hey, Don! Come over here for a minute. I want you to do this job," yells Mr. Schuster.

"All right!" Don hollers above the deafening noise of the machines. He heads over to his boss.

"Come over here." Mr. Schuster directs Don over to an area where a stack of rusty steel beams are laying.

"I want you to sand-blast these. We need them for a project and I want all this rust gone."

He steps over two steel pipes in his way, reaches down and picks up a sand blaster.

"All you have to do, Don, is aim this hose at the rust along the side of these beams. Press this button and the machine pushes sand out of the hose and blasts away at the rust."

Mr. Schuster takes the hose and aims it expertly at a beam that he has already separated from the pile. The loud noise of air going through the blaster to push the sand out of the hose is deafening.

Fussh! Fussh! Fussh!

Mr. Schuster's expert hands aim at the one beam, and blasts the rust off until the area is white. After blasting a few sections, he leaves Don in order to take care of another task.

This is easy enough, Don speculates.

He takes the hose and sets to doing as he was told. After about an hour, he feels satisfied that the ones he's done, have turned out well. He grips the hose and aims it at a spot that needs some more attention. Unexpectedly, a wad of sand ricochets off the beam and hits his finger with such force that the sand rips through his reinforced work glove, pierces his skin and buries itself into the flesh of his left ring finger.

Cuss words pour out of Don's mouth in response to the pain.

He barely gets the blaster turned off without further incident. Shelby, while unloading a pallet of crates, sees Don and rushes over to him.

"Don, are you okay?"

It takes a while for Don to answer because he is still cussing. Don takes off his glove and both men examine the finger.

Shelby lets out his own expletive. "Don, you better go to the hospital right now! Man, that's pretty nasty."

After checking with Mr. Schuster, Don leaves his job for the hospital. On his way, he decides to stop for a drink.

"This finger needs a good shot of whiskey!" he quips.

He spends the rest of the work day, the evening hours, and wee hours of the night at the bar. By the time he leaves, he feels no pain whatsoever.

The next morning he goes to work with a homemade bandage and wards off questions.

"How's the finger, Don?" Shelby asks.

"I'm alright. Don't worry 'bout it. I'm fine," Don replies. He deflects everyone else's inquiry with the same response.

A few days later, his finger, fat with infection, has an abscess the size of a small apricot. Without calling into the job, Don goes to the doctor.

The doctor uses a syringe to pull out the yellow pus and gives Don a prescription for antibiotics.

∞

Now, Don looks at his finger as he sits at Fredrick's bar again. It's been a week since he went to the doctor. He did not fill the prescription and the infection inside the abscess is green in color and his whole hand is swollen, tender, and painful.

The barmaid cannot help but notice. His finger is a disgusting sight. She uses a few colorful words to tell Don what his finger looks like.

"I went to the doctor, but its looks worse now than when I went in." Don attempts an excuse.

A woman, sitting two stools away, overhears their conversation.

"Hey, let me look at it" she beckons to Don. "I'm a nurse over at John Hopkins."

"Sure." Don says dryly.

He extends his hand for her to take a look. The woman looks at the plum-size finger on Don's fat hand and gingerly turns his wrist over.

"Guy, there is a bright red line running from your palm, clear up to your arm-pit. May I touch it?"

"Sure, I don't care."

She gently runs her finger along the line. The small amount of pressure she applies causes Don to fly off the bar stool. The stool falls backwards with a thud.

He curses as he fights to keep his balance and not land beside the stool.

"Guy, you have blood poisoning!" the woman pronounces. "You better go to the emergency room, because if you don't you're gonna pitch over right here." Turning to the barmaid, the woman declares, "He could die right here, I tell you. He's got blood poisoning!"

The barmaid's face gets serious. She is already disgusted.

"Don, you ain't dying in *here*! Get out!"

Don curses at her, "I ain't going nowhere!"

"Get outta my bar right now, Don." she barks. "You ain't dying in here. I mean it!" She stares him down with determined resolve. "Go! Git!"

Don is too drunk to argue and doesn't actually care much. He has already decided out the next bar that he will go to.

Feeling more dejected than his pride wants to admit, he walks across the sticky linoleum floor and goes out the door. He staggers a block east and makes his way into another bar.

As he drinks his first beer, he hears the bartender holler "Is there a Don Johnson here?"

He has never been in this bar before.

Who could possibly be calling me? Don wonders.

"It's me." He raises his voice above the small crowd gathered there.

Don walks around to the side of the bar and picks up the phone.

"Hello," he says quizzically.

Jack, his girlfriend's father, is on the other end.

"Don, it's me. Come over my house right now! I'll drive you to the hospital."

Don replies resignedly, "Okay, Jack. Give me about half an hour."

"This ain't nothin' to play with, Don. Get yourself over here right now!" Jack demands.

Don wonders how Jack heard about his blood-poisoning so quickly and how he knew where he was. A light bulb goes off in his head as he concludes that the barmaid must have watched him stagger down to where he went and then called his girlfriend, Gayle. Gayle is the best thing that has happened to him since Ruth filed for divorced. Now, she had called her dad to make sure that he got his finger taken care of.

Yet, even though he knows that the old man is waiting up for him, Don shows up at Jack's place two hours later.

∞

At the hospital, a nurse looks at his hand, draws some blood, and soon after, the barroom diagnosis is confirmed. A short stocky doctor with glasses and a name tag that says *Dr. Campbell* pulls aside the mustard-yellow curtain that separates the little cubby area where Don sits on a gurney-type bed.

He looks at Don's finger, picks up the chart to read it, and then looks up again at Don.

"Mr. Lucado, I'm going ask a colleague to come and see your finger. It looks like we may have to take it off. If you don't mind, I'd like to have Dr. Patel take a look at it."

The doctor pulls the curtain aside with one clean yank then turns toward the large double doors close by. Don listens to the clicking sound of his heels against the floor tiles as he walks away.

"Take off my finger!" Don exclaims. He looks at Jack who's sitting on the small chair in the corner of the cramped cubby. "What kind of mess is that?"

It was then that he realizes that he is in the same hospital where he had gotten his face "fixed up" the year before.

"I gotta get outta here," he exclaims.

He jumps down from the narrow cot and was about to escape when Dr. Campbell, the new Dr. Patel, and two young and eager interns walk in on him.

"Hi, Mr. Lucado, we're here to look at your finger, okay," Dr. Patel says.

He doesn't wait for Don's reply. He picks up Don's hand and sets it inside his own palm. The two interns and Dr. Campbell move in closer. Dr. Patel touches Don's palm.

"Does this hurt?"

Don winces and nods. "Yes!"

Dr. Patel continues his examination. He asks Don a few more questions before turning away from Don to speak with the others in terms that Don does not understand. Don is feeling increasingly frustrated and even angry. Finally, Dr. Patel turns to look at him.

"Mr. Lucado, if this finger is not amputated, the toxins will attack your entire system more than it already has. We will schedule you for surgery first thing in the morning."

He and the interns march out without saying goodbye. Dr. Campbell turns to look at Don and gives him a faint smile as he too walks away.

A cold sweat breaks out on Don's face.

"Oh God, please don't let them take off my finger," he pleads. He prays another prayer as a back-up to the first. "God, please hear my prayer. Please!"

After twenty minutes of being left alone with Jack and his own fears, Don gets ready to leave. As he reaches for his jacket, a nurse pulls the curtain aside and pushes in a wheelchair.

"Hello!" she greets Don and Jack cheerfully. "We just got an order from Dr. Campbell to postpone your surgery. The doctor wants to give you an antibiotic intravenously and see how you're doing after twenty-four hours."

"Okay, sounds good." Don replies without much expression, but he is relieved.

If he could, he would jump up and click his heels for joy. It takes Don a minute to remember that he had just prayed. *Could this really be an answer to my prayer?* "God, I know you hear me." he says aloud.

He senses that God has not totally forgotten him.

Twenty four hours pass. They cut into Don's finger to drain and clean it. The medication is proving to work well and they do not amputate his finger. However, the skin on the finger is gone and the muscles are atrophied. Don touches the crater in his finger and he feels the bone.

Another day passes and Don's appetite is raging for alcohol. Insignificant things trigger his temper and nothing pleases him. He is nauseous, his limbs tremble, and his intestines feel like they are being emulsified. The only thought Don has is the same thought that he repeats over and over again:

I need a drink. I gotta get outta here.

Don cannot suppress his desire for a drink any longer. He looks at the bandage wrapped around his blue tinged finger.

Aye, this ain't nothing that a few shots of whiskey won't cure.

With that reassurance, he checks out of the hospital despite the doctor's reservations.

On his way out, a nurse clad in white from cap to rubber-soles, hands him a prescription.

"Mr. Lucado, you cannot take this medication and drink alcohol. I'm certain the pharmacist will confirm what I'm telling you. Do you understand me?" She looks at him directly in hopes that he understands what she is telling him.

"If I can't drink alcohol with this medication, I'll just have to self-medicate," Don replies.

He pretends that it's a joke, but both he and the nurse know that he is serious. She gives him a stern look and walks away.

Don leaves the hospital, and goes directly to Cheap Charlie's. When he arrives, he takes a deep breath upon entering the bar.

"It sure feels good to be back," he says to himself.

He grabs a stool with a black plastic cover that has seen better days and scoots it closer to the counter. "Hey, Mona," he greets the bartender without even expecting her to answer back. "Gimme a Budweiser, will ya."

He inhales the familiar smell of the place.

"This is better than the sick hospital smell," he concludes.

He grabs his Budweiser, and as he put it to his lips, he jokes, "If it don't kill me, it'll cure me."

After ten beers, Don begins to feel a buzz. Before he realizes it, the time came for the bar maid to make her nightly announcement.

"Last call, gentlemen. I gotta leave you fine folks and go home to my kids."

Don buys a couple extra beers and takes them to the abandoned building across the alley. He lies down on the grimy checkered tiles of the doorway without noticing the cold and the dirt. He curls up and goes to sleep.

To Don, this is a perfect place to spend the few hours while the bar is closed. It's close by and he can be there again first thing in the morning.

∞

Don spends most of his first week out of the hospital drinking to the extent that he crossed over from the state of drunkenness into sobriety then back into drunkenness again. He hardly gives any thought to his finger. It's not complaining of pain, and at times, he even forgets about it. Several days pass before he takes specific note. To his surprise, and against all human reasoning, his finger has gotten better without him even realizing it. It shouldn't have, but it has. The only one who isn't surprised is his faithful angel companion.

Chapter 12

HIS SECOND HOME

Don walks into the Last Call. It is 8:00 a.m. and many hours have passed since he last saw Doland, the bartender. After several years, Don and Doland have gotten to know each other well.

"Hey you!" Don greets his buddy. "Gimme my whiskey, will you."

Doland pours the whiskey and gives it a little shove so it stops in front of Don.

"Thanks." Don mumbles.

He takes the shot glass in his shaking hands and tries not to spill the precious liquor. Holding it as carefully as he can, he walks over to a round table close to the men's restroom in the rear of the bar. He doesn't like Doland watching him when he is like this.

He sits in his chair and squarely looks at the glass. He puts his two shaking hands around the sides and painstakingly picks it up and attempts to bring it to his lips. Some of the precious fluid spills over onto his hands.

He mutters a cuss word under his breath.

He puts down the glass in order to not spill anymore and decides to make another attempt. However, his hands are shaking so badly that he spills more of what's left in the small glass. Pride aside, he knows what he needs to do.

He puts the glass back on the table and bends his head down towards it. Sticking out his tongue, he dips it repeatedly into the small glass, and laps it up like a dog.

It takes about three shots before Don's hands are steady enough to bring his drink to his mouth. After that, he relaxes by drinking one Budweiser after the next while listening to the same two gospel songs on the old juke box. Somehow, these songs make him feel like God isn't as far away as he sometimes imagines him to be.

∞

"Last call," Doland hollers out at 2:00 a.m. Doland is fond of saying these two words. He likes to hear the name of his bar. As he wipes down the counter with the slippery piece of rag, he glances up at Don.

"Hey, whatcha doing tonight?" he asks.

"I dunno. I can help you clean up, I guess." Don replies.

Doland can always predict what Don will say. If Don could live at the bar, he would. Doland loves getting the free help.

Don didn't plan on going home anyway. He is glad that Doland accepts his offer to stay and help clean up. That's killing one of the four hours until the bar opens again at 6:00 a.m. He anticipates that if he stays inside helping Doland, he might be thanked with a couple of free drinks to hold him over till opening time. He hopes that perhaps he can worm his way into staying in the bar the entire four hours. If not, he will have to go into his car and drink his free drinks in the parking lot. Maybe he will catch a couple hours of sleep.

Don is thankful that he has the old car to sleep in. He remembers a couple months before when he slept in the dark hallway of an apartment building on Wilkins Avenue. He was glad that the passage was carpeted even though the floor was as hard as a rock. Matted with dirt, he had laid his drunken head down to sleep on it, only to wake up with an infestation of fleas.

Don shakes his head at the memory. He now has a new-found sympathy for stray dogs because of that experience.

Don slowly walks toward the back room to get the greasy mop. Opening the musty closet to retrieve the bucket, the smell reminds him of the abandoned row house on Fleet Street. Thinking back, he didn't consider it abandoned since one or two other drunks sometimes stay there. The apartment was furnished with a single queen-size mattress that was brown with stains from dirt, mildew, brew, and body fluids. The other occupants were the city rats whose large size was due to the abundance of garbage that the alley provides for them to feast upon. Don thinks his presence was often a blessing for them. When he stumbled up the steps and dropped his drunken body down on the filthy mattress, the rats were only too pleased to accept the heat his body provided as a refuge from the cold. Often, Don would awaken and see the rats around him. He'd roll over on the mattress or fling his arms and hit more than one. They would squeak and scurry a few feet away, before returning to their bed. There were times when he was glad that he was drunk and tired enough so that he could sleep despite the racket they would make running up and down in the building. To Don, the scampering rats sounded like baseballs rolling down a long flight of stairs. In his present state, he can almost still hear that noise. "SHUT UP!" Don screams out into the dim murky closet.

Doland overhears him. *"Darn drunk!"*

Chapter 13

BETTER OFF DEAD

The rays of the morning sun blast through the holes in Don's blinds. They assault him into waking up even though he doesn't want to. He rolls out of the bed and then sits there with one hand holding the side of his jaw. He is immune to the stench that permeates his apartment. The once cream-colored sheets are walnut-brown from having to suffer Don's hygiene challenges. The air is stale and smells rank. Ashtrays, dirty clothes, empty beer bottles, unopened mail, and some unrecognizable debris are strewn all over his bedroom. The living room and the kitchen counter share the same fate.

Don looks down at his sock-covered feet. He refuses to take off these socks because he knows from experience that if he does, the crusty socks that are meshed onto his feet will peel off bits and pieces of his skin in the process.

Hoisting himself up, he staggers across the room and makes his way to the toilet. He pauses to stare at his reflection in the bathroom mirror. His face is riddled with pockmarks, and alcohol has turned his complexion a pale beet-red. His blue eyes appear black as they look out from two hollow sockets. To Don, black matches the color of his entire world.

He stares back into the eyes that are looking at him and he sees nothing there.

"You are going to die today!" He makes this proclamation to his reflection like he was a judge passing down a death sentence.

"You," he repeats to the emptiness, "are going to die." Then he adds for emphasis, "Today!"

Afterwards, Don goes to the stock pile of ammonia-smelling clothes on the floor in the corner of his bedroom. He fishes through them and chooses a pair of grimy jeans. He picks out a black shirt, strong with odor, but the dirt is less apparent than the others in the pile.

Next, he goes to the kitchen counter and picks up a can of beer. It has just enough in it for him to swish and swirl around his mouth.

Walking out his door, he heads for his 1960 Buick. He misses the van which he used to drive. He had totaled it when he knocked over the telephone pole on Back River Neck Road.

On his way to Last Call, Don sees a large oak tree. It stands majestic as the sole occupant of an otherwise empty lot on the corner of the road. He makes a U-turn in the middle of the street and heads back. Parking his car at the side of the road, he looks intently at the tree. He takes a mental note that the tree standing about ten feet from the edge of the road, has no fence to hinder him from making a sound impact.

Perfect! I'll see you tonight! Don concludes with satisfaction.

Don makes this date with death and he has no intention of missing it. However, to ensure his success, he decides to create a back-up plan. At 9:00 a.m., he pulls up into Last Call and already three of his drinking friends are there. He gets his breakfast which consists of a shot of whiskey and a stick of dried beef jerky.

Around noon, he makes his way from the counter to the little space in the back by the pool table. He looks over each man in the bar as he sizes them up to determine which one could do a thorough job of beating the life out of him.

Donnie dismisses the 5-feet-9-inches-guy. *He ain't big enough.*

He sees a 175-pound man leaning into a girl over by the juke box. *What a wimp! He ain't no good.*

He goes on like this for hours on end.

I need a real man to take me on, not these little weasels he muses to himself.

He wants someone who will knock him out in one punch.

As if on cue, a goliath of a man walks through the door. His imposing build boasts about 280 pounds of muscle strapped onto his six-foot plus-sized frame. The big beer gut that precedes him only serves to make his figure more daunting. His boots thud heavily on the dirty tile floor as he makes his way to the counter. If his stature wasn't enough, his expression tells the fellow patrons that he is not someone to be messed with.

Seeing him, Don smirks with satisfaction. *You are going to kill me today! Right here, right now!*

He waits until the guy finishes two beers before walking over to him.

With a threatening voice, Don challenges the stranger, "Hey, Runt! I'm gonna knock your teeth out!"

Don is not interested in a response. Without further warning, he pulls back his fist and lands a sucker-punch on the side of the giant's face. The man, shocked and dazed, spins around and glares at Don with spit-fire in his eyes.

Don is pleased. He knows that his body is about to take a good beating and hopefully he'll be pounded into the dirt and will be pushing up daisies by tonight.

The menacing man grabs Don by the front of his smelly black shirt. He pulls Don's face within inches of his own and blasts Don with cuss words such as no one has dared to speak to him in years. Don waits for the pain of heavy blows to rain on him, but all he feels is the man's spittle on his face. After saying his piece, the massive man flings Don against the wall.

"Get outta my face, you freaking idiot!" the man shouts in disgust.

He cusses some more, then walks out of the bar leaving Don just as alive as when he had walked in.

∞

Disappointed, Don continues to drink. By evening Don is so drunk that he has crossed back over into sobriety. The bar has turned over a new crowd. The chatter and laughter of young men on dates and gal-friends having their "girls' night out" reminds Don that a place like this can be fun social outlet, just not for him.

At one table along the wall, five young men decide to add to their fun by picking on a soldier one table over. The soldier appears to have just returned from Vietnam and is out having a couple of drinks with his wife.

"Hey, Baby-Killer!" one of the young men shouts. "You ain't got no business in here. Get out."

His buddies laugh at his rude remark.

"Yeah, you ain't got no business over there anyway," another adds.

"Killing those poor people, we don't want you in here."

People, who missed the show that Don had put on earlier, turn around to watch the spectacle. The guys snicker as each tries to upstage the other with off-color remarks.

Despite the harassment, the soldier holds his tongue and doesn't say a word back to them. Perhaps it's because his wife is with him, or perhaps it's the discipline he learned while in the service, or maybe it's because Don has jumped to his defense so quickly that he doesn't need to defend himself.

"Leave him alone!" Don barks, more so to challenge them than to defend the soldier's honor.

"Hey loser, we're just having some fun," one responds.

"We ain't causing any trouble," another one says.

The young men laugh at Don, but they back down. Don turns away dissatisfied with the outcome.

The fellows think that their exchange with Don is over, but Don has other plans for them.

If I'm gonna die, I'm taking these worthless pieces of human garbage with me.

Don waits until 1:30 a.m. and quietly leaves the bar. He sits behind the wheel of his car in the parking lot and watches the door for the guys to make their exit.

At 2:05 a.m., the gang leaves the bar and pulls out onto the street. Don puts his car in gear and follows behind them. They are unaware of what Don has in mind for them until, suddenly; the oversized Buick slams into their rear bumper.

Not knowing whether to pull over or speed up, they decide on the latter, but their clunker can't out-drive the Buick.

Don grasps the wheel, presses on the gas pedal, and aims his car straight ahead.

Wham!

Bam!

With each connection, Don feels a spark of life. Adrenaline kicks in and he feels more alive trying to kill five people than he's felt in years.

"Everybody on this ship is going down tonight." Don says aloud.

Wham! Bam! Wham!

Inside their car, the panicked young men create a hullabaloo of cussing, screaming, begging, and praying. They roll the windows down and holler back at the Buick.

"Stop! Stop!"

But Don is not listening. The guys take a desperate chance, and pull over to the side of the road. The big Buick also pulls over as well and stops several feet in back of them.

"Stop!"

They curse and scream as they holler out of the window. They are too afraid to get out of their vehicle. To them, this is horrifyingly surreal.

After about three long minutes, they venture back onto the road. The Buick creeps up behind them.

Ahead, the road narrows as they head towards the small community of Chase. They have no way of getting off this strip as they approach the overpass. Their minds reel with the thought of possibly sailing over on to Martin Boulevard and crashing down to certain death.

Insanely, Don anticipates greeting his maker. He grips the steering wheel, presses his foot on the gas and prepares himself for the winning impact, when suddenly; he hears God's voice speaking clearly into his heart.

I am going to use you in these last days.

These words are familiar to his spirit and they touch him to his very core.

Immediately, Don slams on the break and stops the Buick in the middle of the road. Without further reasoning, he makes a three point turn, and heads in the opposite direction.

At 3:00 a.m., he drives pass the tree which he marked the previous morning, but he has forgotten all about the appointment that he had made with it.

Chapter 14

EVERY DOG HAS HIS DAY

Don is openly mad at God. He is scared to live and now God has stopped him from killing himself.

"God, why do you tell me that you are going to use me? Look at me! I'm not even a man; I'm an animal."

If Don could have growled like a mad dog he would have in order to prove his point. As far as he is concerned, he has had fleas like a dog, he attacks people like a dog, and he lives like a dog, so he might as well be one. Many people relate to him as if he were a dog. Most, keep their distance when he walks down the street. Nobody sits close to him at the bars anymore. He is a dangerous man, and people know it. Don doesn't blame them; he is even scared of himself.

"Yes, God, I'm an animal. You might as well kill me if you ain't gonna use me. You been trying to kill me since I was born anyway. Why don't you just finish the job?"

Don thinks back to the many car accidents that he's had. To him, they were no accidents. He has been involved in enough of them to think that God is trying to kill him on purpose. Multiple incidents of near death experiences sweep through his mind, and he thinks of the time that his car ended up in a corn field. He will never forget that Saturday night when he was driving too fast and his car skidded on that icy bridge. He'd bounced off a telephone pole, broke through three wooden guard rails, flipped and landed upside down in the field.

Don shakes his head at this memory. While the others around had foreseen the possibility of the car blowing up, and had ran away from danger, he foolishly went back to the car to search for his cigarettes.

He reminisces of other times when he was drunk. Once, he jumped out of Shelby's moving car, breaking his leg in three places. He severed his foot at the ankle and his tibia was completely broken. He curses at the memory.

"God, do you know how many broken bones I have in my body? My hand's been crushed; my head's been split; my legs are pieced together. *You* did this to me!"

Don curses again. He feels disgusted with how broken up his life has become.

His thinking is erratic. He isn't sure whether to blame God or the devil.

"God, you know that Satan's been trying to kill me since I was born."

Don feels so angry that tears spill over onto his cheeks and he wishes that he could spit nails and shoot them into anything or anyone close by. However, he's all alone with nobody to hate but himself.

His mind swoops and dips into hidden places of forgotten memories. He feels the rejection of not having a father, nor being given the name of his real dad. He feels the sadness of having a mother who was too busy with life to show him any special love or validate him as someone important.

He recalls the rape and a sudden swell of nausea sweeps over him.

"Why Lord? Why?" he cries aloud.

"I don't know anybody else who was raped. I don't know anybody else who is bothered by demons who try to suffocate them in the night. I don't know anybody else who is as wretched on the inside as I am right now."

"God, it's all your fault. You are the one in control of all this. You hate me just like everybody else."

∞

While Don wrestles with trying to prevent his mind from going haywire with insanity, three demons are busy shooting darts of poison into Don's mind. Their efforts have been successful but only to a degree, because one determined angel has brought reinforcements and now they are steadily losing ground.

Suddenly, a light breaks through the dark chaos in Don's mind like a ray of sun piercing past stubborn clouds on a stormy day. He thinks about his time in Heaven before he was born. He remembers seeing Jesus and hearing Jesus' promise to him. He questions whether that really happened or whether he'd imagined it somehow. He wonders about his reason for living and dares to hope that perhaps God remembers that time as well.

"Save me, God, save me. If you're ever gonna save me, save me now!"

He cups his head with his large dirty hands and begins to heave in huge deep sobs.

∞

The hot sun beats down on Don as he shuffles down North Point Road to pick up a pack of cigarettes.

"Hey, Don," a voice calls out behind him.

He turns around to see someone whom he hasn't seen in years. It's Larry running to catch up to him.

Oh, Lord, he still runs like a girl.

Larry stops in front of Don trying to bring his breathing back to normal.

"Hey Don," he wheezes.

"What's going on, Larry?"

"Hey, we're having a revival over at our church tonight. Wanna come?"

Don wants to ask Larry whether or not his boyfriend was going to be there too, but he thinks better of it.

Don looks at Larry and somehow Larry seems to have cleaned himself up. His face has a healthy glow and he is smiling and truly looks happy.

"What time?" Don hears himself asks.

Larry beams a little brighter, "seven o' clock."

"Okay," Dons says as he walks away leaving Larry standing on the sidewalk by himself.

"Hey!" Larry shouts after Don, "Bring your girlfriend too. I want yu'all to meet my wife."

Good Lord, Larry really has change!

∞

Being in church is not an unusual experience for Don. As a child, he attended church with his mother, his grandparents, and his Aunt Yelmo. In his own heart, he never left despite how he has been living for the past decades.

In the service, people have their hands raised; they sing and offer praise to God.

"Hallelujah!" the lady next to him declares.

Don looks at her and sees tears rolling down her cheeks. He doesn't feel a single ounce of emotion, but he hopes that God will break through the callousness of his heart and find a tender place. That is, if there is any tender areas left.

"Oh God, meet me tonight," he implores.

During the sermon, Don struggles to concentrate. Suddenly, his mind clears and it seems to him that the preacher is addressing him directly.

"Some of you have known God all your life. You know that He wants to use you, but you've been more ornery than a wild stallion in a corral. How do you expect to be of any use to mankind if you won't let God break you in so you can function and be used in the way He wants to use you?"

Don's ears perk up.

Yes, that's me.

The preacher continues, "I bet you wonder why your life has been a mess. It's because you and other people are messing up God's plan; everyone's living for themselves, hurting themselves and causing other people pain."

The preacher pauses as if to give Don time to think about what he has just said.

"Surrender!" the preacher bellows. "Surrender to God! He brought you into the world and He knows your purpose. Surrender. Surrender. Give Him YOU!"

Don feels a stirring in his heart. He hasn't felt like this in years. He decides to surrender: no wheeling, no deal making, no demanding, and no blaming.

God, I give up. Please don't give up on me. I'm sorry I made a mess of my life.

Tears roll down Don's face.

Under his breath, he pleads, "Can you clean me up, Lord?"

∞

It's a brand new day!

Don wakes up and is immediately conscious of the words that came into his mind. He rubs the sleep from his eyes. The sun seems friendly this morning. The birds are singing and Don feels like singing with them.

I feel like I'm eight years old again. Don muses.

He closes his eyes and sees himself as a child sitting on the swing in the back of his Aunt Nelmo's yard. That day, he had just come from church and the presence of God was more real to him than ever before. He remembers one sweet breeze after another fanning over him as he swayed back and forth on the old swing. Birds were singing more beautifully than he'd ever heard them before, and the sun was kissing his skin. He had never felt so close to God. It was a moment that he will always remember. Now, lying in his bed, he is experiencing the same feelings.

God, thank you for that woman, the only one who ever gave me a real hug. He thinks of the many occasions that his mom sent his away to stay at his Aunt Nelmo's house. He recalls the day when he felt that he should go back home from his extended 'vacation' and had asked his aunt when he could return home. She took him in her loving arms and squeezed him like he was her very own, "Baby, you belong to us now." She said sweetly. Don basked in the pleasantness of her embrace. It wasn't until he was grown before he realized that his long and frequent visits were his mom's attempts at giving him away.

He turns over to see Gayle still asleep. He wonders whether she too will feel as big a difference in her life as he does this morning.

Ring! Ring! The telephone breaks the spell.

Don answers. "Hello?"

"Don," Elizabeth's shaky voice says.

Usually Don hates it when his mother calls, but this morning, listening to her is tolerable.

"Don, I'm going to an Ernest Ainsley revival meeting tonight. I was wondering if you can give me a ride there."

"Sure," Don says, not believing that he has just agreed to take his mother to a revival meeting. The last time he saw Elizabeth, she was in her rocker on the little porch of her trailer. "Don, is that you?"

she called out as he passed by. Don knows that his mother's cataracts makes everything she sees a blur. He walked by without saying a word or even looking in her direction.

∞

Don likes the meeting more than he cares to admit. He feels an unexplained kinship with the people there. Two hours turn into three, before Don realizes it.

Ernest Ainsley speaks. "1984 is a good year to have a fresh start. I'm talking to all who need help with their drug addictions. Are you addicted to alcohol, heroine, or cigarettes? God wants to set you free tonight."

Suddenly, Don feels an overwhelming urge to go outside and smoke a cigarette.

"Mom, I'm going outside; be right back."

He practically runs into the lobby to light his cigarette.

Taking a deep puff, he thinks, *This tastes so good.*

Soon, he lights another one.

By the time he gets back inside, there is a crowd gathered down by the podium. The choir is singing softly.

Without Elizabeth questioning him, he defensively declares, "Mom, I'll go down there next time."

Ernest Ainsley is still speaking. Don listens intently.

"All the ones who didn't come forward, I want you to know that God wants to meet you right where you are. Today is your day too. Every dog has his day, and today is your day. Why don't you close your eyes and repeat after me."

Don believes in his heart that God is telling him that today is indeed his day. He closes his eyes and repeats after the servant of God.

"Dear God, I need you. I can't save myself from my addictions. I can't save myself from my sins. You know I can't, that is why You sent your Son to die on the cross. He died so I wouldn't have to. God, I'm tired of killing myself with my sins and with my addictions. Please save me, Lord. I want Jesus. I want Your way and not mine. Please take all of me today and make me a new person. In Jesus' Name. Amen."

Chapter 15

HELL IS REAL

"Don, you going to church this morning?" Gayle asks as she rolls over and flings her right arm across Don's chest.

"It's Sunday, Babe."

Don feels that he doesn't have to say any more because neither he nor Gayle has missed going to Church for the past sixteen Sundays since he went to that Ernest Ainsley revival meeting. In fact, he usually can't wait for Sundays to come. He remains in a state of constant awe that he hasn't had a drink or even one cigarette since then.

Don bounds out of bed.

"Time to hit the shower!"

Gayle sits up and looks at him as he fidgets around to find a clean pair of underwear.

"Don, we gonna get married or what?"

"What are you talking about, Gayle? This ain't the time, Babe."

"But Don...."

Don interrupts her before she can say anything further. "Gayle, we'll talk about that later, okay. Now, hurry up girl, before we're late."

He rushes into the bathroom to avoid any further discussion with Gayle.

"Lord, I hear You talking to me. I ain't gonna marry her Lord, but I know I can't be shacking up with her either."

Soon, Don and Gayle are sitting in the car, each lost within their own thoughts. They arrive at church and both can hardly wait to get inside to connect with God and pray that He makes His perfect will clear to them.

∞

Don cherishes his sleep especially on nights like tonight when his body is aching and his lower back is screaming for pain killers.

"Gayle, can you rub some *Ben Gay* on my back?" he asks.

Before long, Gayle is practicing her best massage techniques.

"You guys still hanging beams down at that building?"

"Yeah, and it's killing me. I'm just not a spring chicken anymore Gayle," Don mumbles.

"How's this?" Gayle pushes down near Don's coccyx bone with the heel of her hand.

She waits for a reply, but Don is already dead to the world.

∞

In the dark hours of the night, Don becomes conscious of rapidly plunging down a narrow hole leading to the middle of the earth. Having no control over the matter, he suddenly finds himself in Hell. He lands in a "waiting room" and immediately gets the understanding, by some means, that this "room" is where people wait for their punishment and for their permanently assigned place in Hell.

Beyond the room, everywhere is engulfed in flames and smoke.

Overcome with fright, Don desperately wails, "Oh God! Help me!"

A partition of smoke separates Don from the rest of Hell, but he is still able to see the horrors of various parts of the place.

One of the first things Don sees is a wall made up of a mortar and grassy substance. Buried within are body parts moving against each other. To his horror, he realizes from the body parts, that actual people are jammed together. He witnesses a contortion of humanity worming their way into this wall to avoid the flames.

Mentally, he becomes conscious of these words, *These people in the wall just left this room you're in. They are going to be taken from there to the areas where they will be permanently placed.*

Suddenly, horrific-looking demons of various shapes and sizes with long razor-sharp talons and fang-like teeth began pulling screaming people from the packed wall. They sink their teeth into the humans' shoulders and necks, grappling their flesh like hungry lions ripping apart prey. At times, like a cat that toys with a mouse, the demons release their grip. The people attempt to dart into the fire to get away or run back and bury themselves deeply into the wall, and pray that they won't be tortured by the demons anymore. The demons grab them again, laugh, and throw them back down.

Don never thought that the sound of laughter could ever be horrible, until he hears a group of demons laugh. He looks to see them laughing at a witch who is boasting about how much she had served Satan while she was alive. They laugh as they rip and break her into pieces then smash her bones. Yet, they could not kill her; her body parts came back together for them to shred her to bits over and over again.

Looking away from that scene, Don sees a vast mountainous landscape with sharp peaks blazing in flames of orange and red. He realizes that this far-reaching, ever-extending landscape is not a formation made from rock or earth, but rather, from an uncountable number of people compacted together. Bodies create these mountainous slopes. Eyes and mouths emit fire, while flames cover bodies without consuming them.

Don's senses are past overload. His brain registers a measure of fear which he has never known before. He stands taking in the unbelievable sights, the repugnant smell of burning flesh and filth, and the sound of continuous roaring generated by a combination of prayers, screams, fearful voices, cries, shrieks and the hammering of hands hitting burning flesh that refuse to be consumed by fire. Overcome with fright, Don screams and screams and screams.

∞

Before sunrise, Don becomes aware that he is in the land of the living. Realizing that he is alive again, and that his time in Hell is over, he convulses into sobs of appreciation.

"Thank you, Jesus! Thank you, Jesus!"

The name of Jesus is the only word Don's speaks for minutes on end.

"Jesus! Jesus! Jesus!"

He wants to tell Gayle what happened to him but each time he opens his mouth all he can say is, "Jesus! Jesus! Jesus!"

Gayle, now awake from the racket Don is making, watches him as he runs around the apartment hollering for joy.

Finally, Don tells Gayle what happened to him.

"Gayle, I died last night and went to Hell!"

Gayle looks at Don in disbelief. He tells her about the fire and the wall packed with people and the demons and the witch.

Don tells her more of what he saw, "Gayle, Hell is a sea of bodies. It's so packed that sometimes it was hard to distinguish one person from the masses. Once in a while, I would recognize something such as a face or a hand in the flames. I could hear some of the words that people were saying. 'Get it off of me. Please get it off of me. Get it off, get it off please.' They were screaming. They were hitting their bodies trying to knock the fire off, but the fire would only get bigger each time they tried to brush it off".

Gayle stares at Don with her mouth agape in surprise. "Gayle, I know this is hard to believe, but I saw children in Hell. Children were burning and screaming like the adults. I saw children who shot other children getting sprayed with bullets that rip their bodies apart. Their flesh would seal back together so more bullets could rip through them again. Their screaming was horrible, Gayle. They cried out for their moms and for their dads. They cried out to Jesus. They pleaded and begged, but there was no one to help them."

Needing to get ready for work, Gayle gets up and goes to the closet to get some clothes.

"Go on babe, I'm listening."

"Gayle, I saw people who were like glass filled with fire. Really, they were transparent. They were nothing but fire."

Gayle looks at the digital clock on the night stand.

"Babe, I have to get ready for work. But tell me, if you died, Don, how did you come back?"

Don chokes up just remembering. He doesn't know whether Gayle believes him or not, but he doesn't care.

"Why God allowed me to go to Hell and see this Gayle, is beyond me. But he allowed me to see the things I saw from that waiting room. I ain't never been so scared in all my life. The worst part was when it was my own judgment time. I heard a voice say, 'YOU ARE NOT WORTHY OF THE KINGDOM OF HEAVEN!' That was God, Gayle! That was God! As soon as I heard that, I saw one demon about 3-feet tall high-tailing it towards me, I knew that I was toast. It's like he was waiting a long time for me *personally* and he was released by God to come and take me. He cussed at me and called me terrible names. He was telling me that he was going to tear me apart. All of a sudden, I heard a voice coming out of the smoke. It said, 'PRAY NOW! Once across the gulf, your prayers will not be heard! Once across, you can never return.' Oh gosh, Gayle, I dropped to my knees and pleaded to Almighty God. 'Forgive me God! Forgive me! Oh God, give me another chance, please!' Gayle, I never prayed so hard in my life. That demon was just about to grab me before I came back into my body."

"Honey, you just had a bad dream," Gayle consoles.

"No, Gayle. I died. This wasn't just a dream. I was in Hell for real!" Don insists.

Don is visibly shaking. He doesn't care whether Gayle believes him or not. Gayle steps close to him and gives him a kiss on his cheek.

Don calms down a little.

"Gayle, I've been playing with God. I live with one foot in the world and one foot in Church. No more, Gayle, no more. I'm not shacking up with you. I know you love God too and want to live right. I'm making the decision, Gayle. I'm giving God everything I've got. I'm giving God all of me."

"Amen!" Gayle says, as she thinks the very same thing.

Chapter 16

THE FORTY-DAY FAST

*F*orty Days! These two words settle clearly into Don's mind like a breeze blown purposefully upon his consciousness. He has been asking God about how long he is to be on this new fast. God answered his prayer.

Forty days, Lord? Don asks this question as he straightens up from untying the shoe-laces of his dirty work boots.

"God, You will have to give me the strength to do this." This is the second time that God told Don in no uncertain terms, and he knows for sure that this is the answer to his prayer.

"God, I know that I can do twenty-seven days, but I can't do forty." As soon as the words came out of his mouth, Don decides that he should take a different course in the conversation. "Tell you what, God, I'll do one day at a time." Their understanding was sealed.

Don is no stranger to fasting. He begins to reflect back upon the last long-term fast that he did. It was for twenty days. He has fasted on many occasions since then, but it was those twenty days that had accelerated a supernatural change to his character and to his spiritual life. "Oh Lord, You are faithful to me. You took me through that, You will take me through these forty days too. After all, Lord, You did forty days; Moses did forty days; He was a man like me and You helped him; I know that You will help me too."

Don bends down again, finishes untying his boot, grabs it by the heel and flings it over into the corner of his bedroom. His mind goes back to his grandfather, as it usually does at times like these. He believes that his grandfather's passion for God, led him to live a life where fasting was a common occurrence in his spiritual life. Don closes his eyes to see if he could recreate a mental image of his grandparents. He never knew when grandpa was fasting until perhaps at mealtimes when he was absent from the table. He remembers the times when Grandpa was missing from the dinner table, and how he had asked his grandma where Grandpa was. It was only at those times when his grandmother would simply state, "He is fasting," and that was all she needed to say. Don reaches down for the other boot, wrestles it off his foot and tosses it so it lands next to the first. He had watched his grandpa make regular trips inside his prayer closet. Now Don frequents his own prayer closet. He emptied out the bottom of the tiny area, clearing the floor before going inside the cramped space. Once, he closed the door on his head. *That hurts.* Don chuckles.

Don remembers how his grandfather's prayers work the time when he had a fever so high that it made him delirious. His grandfather's hands felt like ice to him when he touched him and prayed, "Lord, heal this child. Take his fever and cast it to the pit of hell. Let this child live to give you glory. I thank you, Lord. In Jesus' Name. Amen." Don smiles as he remembers the next day when he was outside playing and running around in the best of health. "Lord, thank You for giving me godly grandparents," he declares aloud. It is the memory of his grandfather's prayers and fasts that God uses to encourage him in his new walk of faith. Years before, when he had done the twenty-seven days of fasting and prayer, he felt closer to God than he had ever felt in a very long time. He felt like God was so close that he could touch Him. He hopes this experience will have a similar impact.

Tears begin to well up in Don's eyes as he feels overwhelmed by the love that God has shown to him.

Lord, you are so merciful.

Don spreads his fingers and combs his hands over his scalp. His greasy hair is ready for a wash just as much as he is. He pushes down on his head as he recalls that it has been over a decade since that twenty-seven-day fast. He had surrendered his life over to God for several months prior, and he was still shacking up with Gayle. Both he and Gayle were very serious about serving the Lord but neither one had surrendered to the conviction that cohabitating and engaging in an intimate relationship outside of marriage, is sinful. Don shakes his head in amazement and wonders how in the world God worked it out so that he and Gayle had separated without malice or ill-intent. Now, years later, she and her husband live in the trailer right beside his. *God, you are so good.*

The next day, Don is still thinking about what God said to him the evening before. Some dust from the sheetrock that he is hanging falls on his shoulders. He fits the sheetrock alongside the one which he just secured onto the wooden beam before addressing the Dominican beauty he's worked beside for the last four years.

"Nina, God told me something."

Nina, now accustomed to Don telling her that he hears from God, responds without much fanfare.

"Oh yeah?" She sweeps her eyes around the work area as if to determine whether God showed up on the scene without her realizing it. "What'd He say?"

"He just told me how long I'm gonna fast for."

"How long?"

"I can't tell you yet, but it's a long time. I'm gonna need your help."

Nina doesn't always understand Don, but she knows that he is a sincere guy and that she likes him a lot.

"Sure, Don. Just let me and Lillian know what's going on, okay. We have your back."

Don restrains himself from leaning over and kissing Nina fully on the lips. He feels happy just to be sharing paint stains with someone with such a caring heart. The fact that he is secretly in love with Nina only serves to heighten her status of sainthood in his eyes.

"Thanks, Nina."

To Don, working with these two sisters, plus having Andy as his boss is definitely a way that God has smiled on him. Not everyone has a boss who is a strong Christian man and one who understands about such a spiritual discipline as fasting.

Lord, when I asked You how long this fast was going to be, I didn't think You'd say forty days. I know You will take me through it and I know You will talk to Andy for me.

Before leaving for the day, Don decides that it is best to tell Andy what he is about to do. He knocks on the gray steel door of the trailer and steps into the musky office. He smells the coffee and glances at the scorched liquid in the brown-stained coffee-pot. He turns his attention to the small water cooler a couple of feet next to him, grabs a cup, and fills it up.

"Andy, I gotta tell you something."

Andy looks up at Don smiling like he has just heard a joke and was still getting pleasure from this private humor. Seeing Andy's expression, Don lets out a breath and his body relaxes a little. As Don relates his story, he notices Andy's face and realizes that though Andy is patiently listening to what he has to say, a look of concern is steadily registering on his face.

Don tries to reassure him. "Don't worry, Andy. I'm still going to be putting in my days. God will give me the strength."

"Don, I'm more worried about you than work. Right now we don't have too many jobs coming in anyway." He pauses before continuing, "You sure you heard from God?"

"Yes. I wouldn't do this on my own. I *can't* do this on my own." Don wanting to end the conversation on a good note says, "Just pray for me okay."

"If you're sure that this is what God told you to do, well, I'll be praying for you." Andy gives Don a faint smile. "Just let me know what's going on with you, okay?"

Andy puts his head down and begins to look at some paperwork. Don takes the cue that the meeting is over. He walks out of the trailer feeling relieved.

∞

Don does not have a fasting plan. He decides that he will have water. Coffee is the only other drink that comes to his mind. He feels peaceful about drinking that, but apart from just winging it one day at a time, the only other thing he thinks of, is to mark 'X's on the calendar so that he can keep track of the days.

He goes to Sam's Club and stocks up on cases of water. He stores them against the small counter that separates the tiny kitchen from the living room in his small trailer.

On day one, Don has a cup of black coffee and water; this sets the standard for the many days to follow. The first few days are pretty much what he expects. He experiences some hunger pangs and some dizziness which he knows will leave. By week two, he feels grateful to have Mina and Lillian. Having to work while fasting, is taking its toll.

"Here, Don. I'll carry that for you." Mina reaches over and grabs the five-pound paint bucket out of Don's hand.

"Thanks, Mina. If you can bring the ladder over here for me, I'll set it up."

Mina has already decided that she and Lillian will paint all the molding along the ceiling so that Don won't have to climb up on the ladder. She saw him stumble across the floor earlier but pretended that she didn't. She doesn't want to take the chance of him losing his balance.

"Don, why don't you do the baseboards? Me and Lillian will paint the molding."

"Okay. Sounds good to me," Don chuckles at her.

They both know that he is happy with this decision. Don's walking is growing increasingly sluggish. It takes energy for him to properly lift his feet off the ground. He isn't driving anymore either, mainly because his thinking isn't as clear and sharp as it used to be. Now, Mina and Lillian drive the van.

"Hey, Don," Lillian says, "Andy was asking for you earlier. He wants to talk to you."

"Uh-Oh," acknowledges Don.

Soon, Don is standing in Andy's little office.

"Hey, Brother Don, tell me the truth. How are you doing?" Andy asks the question because he is concerned about Don. Don has obviously dropped some weight. He can scarcely give a decent handshake. Don looks across the crowded metal desk to where Andy is sitting. Sometimes he wonders how Andy can find anything amidst this pile of mail, papers, and tools. Right now, he doesn't much care about something so insignificant as clutter, because he is truly hurt that he is unable to do his job. He realizes how foolish he was to think that God would give him supernatural strength to do his job.

"Andy, I'm okay. I'm just weak, you know."

"Don I didn't think that you'd make it this long on the job. Go ahead home. When it's over, come back to work."

Tears roll down Don's face. "It breaks my heart to leave my job Andy. I just gotta right now."

He leaves Andy's office feeling like the bottom has just fallen out from his world.

∞

Don cannot go to work but he certainly will not miss church, if he can help it. Pastor Reynolds at the Full Gospel Church where Don attends is going to host their Full Gospel Television program this Sunday after the service. The television program is taped from a set that Don, Andy, and others, built on the second floor of the church building. The set consists of a raised platform constructed out of plywood and is covered over with maroon-colored carpet. It has two love seats, two plastic Fica trees and a shiny wooden coffee table to make it look like a sweet little living room setting.

During the taping, Pastor Reynolds, Don, and two other men from the congregation are seated and having a lively conversation. Pastor Reynolds likes to have people share testimonies of what God is doing in their lives in order to encourage others. Towards the end of the program, Pastor Reynolds turns his attention to Don.

"Don, won't you tell us what the Lord has been doing in your life lately." The camera closes in on Don's face.

Don looks at Pastor Reynolds; his deep voice is raspy but clear. "God has been dealing with me about fasting. I've been on a fast because God told me to go on a fast."

"Why do you thinking fasting is important, Brother Don?"

"Fasting is one of the things that God uses to get us closer to him. Jesus fasted for forty days. He did that before he started his ministry."

"How long are you fasting for?"

"Forty days, because God told me to."

"Hallelujah! We have to listen to the Lord. Don't we?"

"Amen, we have to listen *and* obey the Lord, Pastor Reynolds."

"Amen!" Pastor Reynolds declares as he wraps up his conversation. As they close their program, he looks directly to the cameras and smiles. "Well, don't forget that we'll be coming to see you soon. Please stay tuned for further details."

Don is not camera-shy, but he is relieved that he was not asked any personal questions about his fasting because there are some things which he could never share. For instance, he is losing control of his bladder. It's getting to where he is seriously considering walking around with a bottle because he isn't making it to the bathroom in time. Also, he has been experiencing pangs of pain that make him cry out, and his legs muscles contract into painful cramps. These things are too personal. God knows and that is enough.

This is his second time on the church's television program and now everyone knows that he is fasting for forty days.

By week five, Don's children are getting worried, even afraid. Don looks like he has lost about fifty pounds. A concerned Melissa confronts her father.

"Dad, what's wrong with you. You have cancer?"

"No. I'm fasting."

"Dad, stop it now! Your heart is bad; you can't fast like this. We need you here. You're dying."

"Melissa, I'm okay." Don says dismissively.

"Was I the only one in the office when the doctor told you that you had a bad heart?" Melissa looks at him in disbelief as she asks the question. "Didn't the doctor say that your heart was beating so slowly that they were setting to put you in the hospital?"

Melissa's face is turning redder by the second. Don doesn't need her reminders. Last month, the EKG showed that his heart was in serious trouble. The doctors were talking surgery and a pace-maker. The hospital even had a bed waiting for him.

Everyone else but him thinks that is a serious diagnosis. Rather than taking this prognosis seriously, he's put off attending to it by telling everyone, "I'll go after the first of the year." His family is very upset at him. They don't want him to come to the Christmas party because they are angry at him.

Now he sees Melissa's concern and realizes that he is the only one who is not worried. He knows his heart is bad, but he has faith that God will keep him alive.

Don doesn't have the strength to argue with her. He is glad to see Ruth walking across the lane to join them. Ruth joins in on the conversation, "Melissa, leave him alone, God will protect him."

Don agrees with Ruth, "Yes, Melissa, God will protect me. I tell you, baby girl, I'm all right." Don silently thanks God that Ruth returned from Florida and is now living in the same trailer park.

Don is tired of hearing people tell him that he is dying. He really appreciates that Ruth has confidence in God and is helping him strengthen his own faith.

"Thanks, Ruth."

∞

Knock. Knock.

Don hears the sound but has no intention of going to the door.

"Mr. Lucado! Mr. Lucado?" Don painstakingly stretches his arm out to pull aside the curtain of the living room window. He sees the mailman.

"Hold on," Don raises his voice the best he can and slowly lifts himself up from off the couch.

It takes him several seconds to reach the door even though it is only a couple feet from the sofa. He opens it to see the mailman standing there matter-of-factly.

"Here you are, Sir. Sign right here." The mail-man hands Don a pen and as he points to the X on the line of the paper pinned down to his clip board. Don painstakingly reaches out and takes the pen. Suddenly, he draws a blank. He cannot remember how to write his name. His explores long forgotten places within his brain.

Don...Oh Gosh! How do you spell Don? He looks at the mail-man in puzzlement. He cannot remember the shapes of the letters in the alphabet. If he asks the mailman to tell him how to spell his name, the mailman will also have to show him what a "d" looks like. It takes Don an embarrassing moment of fumbling, before he remembers how to write his name.

Before the mailman leaves, he hands Don the stack of letters that he has for him. Don is grateful. Yesterday, when he walked the several yards to where the mailboxes are across the lane, it took him ten minutes. While he was walking, he felt like he was moving at a normal pace. At times, he even felt like he was hurried in his steps, but later on, he realized that he was going at a snail's pace, because it doesn't normally take a person ten minutes to walk several yards.

Don knows that going outside is not something that he will be doing much longer. He thinks of Melissa and how worried she is about him.

He also remembers that his neighbors, Gayle, and her husband, Lonnie, already told him that they were uncomfortable when he comes over to their trailer. The other day, Gayle was kind enough to be honest with him. "Don, what can I tell you? You got the odor of death on you." Don was shocked that Gayle was so blunt. Gayle continued in the kindest voice she could, "Trust me Don, after working with all them people in the nursing home, I know what I'm talking about."

Lonnie chimed in, "We love you, Don, but we don't want you dying over here."

No sir, I'm not going back outside these doors. Don thinks to himself. *God, I can't make it listening to all these people. You told me that I will not die but live and that I will be your prophet in these last days. I know I'm gonna make it.*

∞

"Agh!" Pain grips Don's body and wakes him up after only three hours of sleep. His muscles tighten. He feels like a pair of giant pliers are gripping and squeezing his insides. He wants to hold his head, but his arms are tightly bent against his bony chest, his wrists are forced under, with his fingers balled into a fist that he cannot unclench. His thigh and leg muscles are cramping simultaneously. As the pain grabs him, he hoarsely calls out, "God! God!" His cotton-coated tongue is lodged in place as he cries, "God! God!"

Don isn't thinking straight; he isn't sure how well his brain is working. He only knows that it feels like it is stuck to the roof of his skull. His eyelids even feel stuck to his eyeballs. Feebly, Don pleads, "Lord, please take me."

"Oh God! Oh God!" he moans, "Let me die, Lord. I know you'll bring me back. I just need to rest for a while!" He passes out just minutes later.

Ring! Ring! Ring!

The telephone causes Don to stir. He knows not to move too quickly; if he does, he might cramp up again.

Ring! Ring! Ring!

Who's calling at this time of the morning? he wonders.

Don finally stretches to where he can pick up the phone and put it to his ear. "Hello," his bull frog greeting is met with a near-panicked voice on the other end.

"Dad, where have you been? We haven't seen you in days! What's going on?"

"Melissa, I'm fine. I'm staying by myself for a while. I told you. Didn't I?"

"Dad, how are you? You sound terrible."

"I'm okay. Just let me be."

He successfully puts the phone back on the cradle after two attempts. He slowly raises himself up and off the bed.

Don smells himself but doesn't much care. He is getting used to rolling out of a pee-soaked bed. *Man, I wish I knew when I peed last night.* His bladder lets loose while he sleeps without signaling him. He gets up and shuffles himself to the bathroom. "Lord, I think I'll make it this time," he half-jokes to himself as he remembers the warm liquid running down his leg yesterday. He looks at the toilet bowl like it's a foreign object and stands over by the sink instead. The yellow stream whirlpools around the hole at the base of the sink before slowly draining down. Don turns on the faucet, lets the water run over his hands, and wipes his wet hands on his face.

As he turns into the doorway, he feels his heart flutter. Then, it forcibly jumps against his chest. On previous occasions, he has felt his heart skip a couple beats, but this is the first time that he actually sees his heart move against him chest.

"Lord, my heart is in your hands." He takes a few deep breaths. "My heart will safely trust in you Lord. I give my heart to you." This is all Don says to quench the shock of actually seeing his heart jump.

∞

Don isn't looking forward to seeing a new day. He is scared and he feels an ache of desperate loneliness. Inwardly he prays. *Lord, I wish I know what is going to happen to me today. I wish I know someone else who fasted this long so they can tell me what is going to happen to me next. I don't know what other kinds of pain are going to hit me today, Lord. I'm scared. Please don't leave me alone.*

Don isn't feeling the presence of God like he used to and he is terrified. This fast is not turning out as he thought it would. *How is it possible to feel so alone?* He thinks of Jesus and feels that he has an idea of the degree of the pain, and loneliness that Jesus must have felt when He didn't feel His Father's presence. His mind begins to think of the pain of Jesus' crucifixion and concludes that the most horrible pain that Jesus must have felt was when He too could not feel His Father's presence. Jesus had said, "My God, why have You forsaken me," and Don wants to say the same thing as well.

Don has not heard from God and he doesn't know why. Despite that, he still talks to God. He drags his feet over to the calendar hanging on the wall leading into the bedroom and uses a black marker to make his "X". *Four more days to go.*

He begins his usual one-way conversation with God.

"God I can't stop until forty, but God I'm so alone. Where are You?" Don remembers hearing that the Bible doesn't record that the Father spoke with Jesus while he was going through his trials leading to Calvary. He takes a measure of comfort in that knowledge.

Don sits on the bed and puts his face in his hands and starts to sob, "Jesus, Jesus, I'm so alone. I'm so alone."

Unexpectedly, a clear whisper registers on his mind and into his heart. *That's what I felt.*

Four small words, but Don's insides swell up. He soaks in the presence of God. He basks in the feeling that God is still with him. He prays, "Oh Jesus, I love You. I love You. I love You."

A wonderful peace comes over Don and as he lays down on the smelly sheets, he thinks, *I am God's prophet and He is going to use me in these last days.* He puts his hope in these words.

Chapter 17

THE REASON WHY

Praise fills the church. Don sings along with the worship and praise team and the rest of the congregation.

"Our God is an awesome God. He reigns from Heaven above. With wisdom, power, and love, our God is an awesome God!" The song ends and everyone claps their hands. The applause is loud and several voices can be heard above the noise.

"Amen!" "Hallelujah!" "Praise the Lord!"

In the midst of high praise, Don's thoughts go to his mom. Don sobers at the memory of him sharing one of his stories at his mom's funeral. He remembers how his mom would usually walk out of the room or purposely interrupts him when he tried to tell some of the stories that God often inspire him to record. Don feels a distinct pain in his heart. *I finally got you to listen to one of my stories mom; you couldn't leave the room. Could you?*

As he thinks about his mom, he can't tell if his pain is from hurtful memories or from the fact that she has recently died. *Mom, I know you were old, but who dies from three kinds of cancer? I told you to go to the doctor.* Don knows that Elizabeth who had hardly ever been to a doctor in her eighty six years of life didn't care to start making it a habit now that she was at such a ripe old age. She usually said, "God's taking care of me; don't worry none." Don smiles. It is as if he can still hear her voice. He thinks back upon one of the last words that she had spoken to him before she died. "Don," Elizabeth had said, "I heard you speak to me when you were in my stomach." Surprised at Elizabeth's unprovoked declaration, Don instinctively asked, "What did I say?" But Elizabeth closed her eyes and spoke nothing else.

Strange as her words were, Don was not surprised. He had often told his mother that he remembers being in her stomach. He didn't realize before then, that she had believed him all along.

Don raises his hands and starts singing along with everyone.

The worship team begins playing the prelude to the next song. Don closes his eyes as the sound reaches his ears, washing away his memory of his mom and bringing him to a place of joy. Unexpectedly, the most unusual scene comes to the forefront of his mind. He sees a terrible earthquake in a big city filled with huge structures and tall buildings. Above it all, a gigantic number, seven, was painted across the sky. On the ground, the streets are packed with people going about their daily activities. Cars, SUVs, trolley cars, and taxis run along the streets. The main thing that catches Don's attention is a gigantic split along the ground. A thunderous rumble and great shaking topple tall buildings in a matter of seconds. People disappear inside wide gaping openings in the earth.

The mass hysteria and confusion is amazing in itself, but these images are only minor events. Don focuses on the massive split. It looks like a long train track along the ground. Don judges it to be about a block wide. There is total blackness in the deep crevice. It doesn't seem to have an end, but he knows the name of city it starts in and he knows where it ends. Its destination was Sin City.

This image leaves just as quickly as it came. Don knows that he couldn't have invented the vision that he just experienced. His heart feels full with the presence of the Lord. He opens his mouth and begins to sing with the congregation, *"How great is our God."*

Don prays, "Yes, God. You are great."

∞

Don is excited as he rings the doorbell of his sister Pat's house. Pat pulls her living room curtain back to see Don standing there with a shy grin on his face. Don wonders how it can be that though he and Pat both live within miles from each other; they don't spend much time together. Don reminds himself, *You were meaner than a snake Don, no wonder you're not close to your family.* He hears Pat's grown kids playing music from one of the upstairs bedrooms as she opens the door.

"Whatcha doing here?" Pat asks.

"Nothing. Just came by. That's all."

"Umm. So, what's going on?"

Don is not very good at making small talk and is relieved that he has an open door to tell Pat all that was going on with him. He mostly loves talking about the special things which he feels that God is showing him.

Don enters the small living room. Pat sits across from Don in her comfy recliner and prepares herself to hear one of Don's fantastic stories. She knows that her brother loves to talk.

"Pat, let me tell you what God showed me last night. You would not believe this! I saw a gigantic tidal wave wipe out the entire East Coast of this country. I mean the entire East Coast from way up north to all the way down south." Don's voice increases in volume and animation as he tells his vision.

"I saw the water rise up so high into the sky that it looked like a giant white cloud was rising up from out of the water to the heavens. It just pushed out of the water like an atomic blast and covered everything inland. I'm telling you, Pat, it wiped out the entire East Coast."

Pat leans forward, "Don, that sounds like a tsunami!"

"Yep. That's it. A giant tidal wave." He continues, "You know, Pat, last month I was sitting in church thinking about mom and everything, when I saw a vision of an earthquake. Man, that was something else! You know, God told me that I am His prophet for these last days. I use to be so sheepish and so insecure about myself. But now, I just say, '*Here I am, Lord. Use me!*'"

"The month before that, God showed me that this *big* country is going to have three smaller countries gang up on it, to take it down."

"Yes, you started to tell me about that the other day. I didn't quite get it."

"Yeah. I watched a country that is so big that no other country wanted to fight them alone so they had to form an alliance. Three countries made this pact to join together to bring it down. They attacked it on the eastern, southern and western part of this country."

Pat listens intently. She doesn't need Don to tell her the name of the big country. She is sure that she has already heard this story before or something close to it.

"What happens when they attack this country?" Pat inquires.

"This country began going to its bordering countries. In turn, those neighbors denied them entrance saying, 'If we let you in, their alliances will attack us.'"

"Do you know why they would attack this country? The alliance attacks this country because it's friends with a much smaller country. They hate this small country in the Middle East and they know that this giant would defend it. So it's like getting the big brother before they pick on the little brother."

Pat appreciates Don's passion for spiritual things. She is always guaranteed a good story when Don is around. She thinks of their brother's death several years back and wishes he could see how Don has changed. *Too bad Shelby isn't here to see what's going on in your life Don.* She muses.

She wants to hear more of what Don has to say.

"Speaking of the Middle East, what were you telling me the other day about what God showed you about the Dome of the Rock?"

Don grows more and more animated. He is about to jump out of his seat.

"Oh yeah, I saw the ground underneath the Dome start to shake. It was an earthquake. The entire building fell flat to the ground. Then, flames combusted and consumed the thing. The next thing I saw was a pile of ashes after the fire. After that, a huge wind came and blew the ashes away."

Pat wants to ask a question, but Don has one of his own. "You know *who* did that, Pat? *God* did that, Pat. God told me that He did it so the world will know that it was His hand that did this and not man!"

"Wow!" Pat exclaims.

Don continues, "I watched it like it was a movie. Satan's trying to kill me because this is what God put me here to do. The devil's been trying to kill me for as far back as I can remember, but I know that God put me here for a reason. These things are going to happen. God shows me so much and tells me so much, Pat. I'm His prophet and I want the people to know that these things are coming."

Pat can tell that Don is impassioned about this subject. The music upstairs competes for her attention, so she makes eye contact to show her interest.

Don continues, "God told me the story of the Dome of the Rock and how it would be destroyed, and all that. God told me why the Dome of the Rock had to be destroyed too. It's because they have to build the temple. A temple must be built, even if there is bloodshed, because when God comes back, He is going to use the temple."

Don looks at Pat with a big grin and rubs his upper arms with his hands as if warding off a chill.

"Pat, God tells me things all the time. He shows me a lot. I'm so happy when He speaks to me. Oh, I feel His presence all over me. I wish you could feel what I'm feeling. Oh! God is awesome."

Pat isn't quite sure that she believes all that Don is telling her, but she knows that her brother simply loves God.

"Yes, Don, God is awesome."

∞

Don's guardian angel smiles.

"There is more work to be done, my charge, but you are walking on the right path. You will face many more challenges in life but know that there are bright horizons ahead. You will grow with God and He will use you in mighty ways to show His love to others. Stay close to Him, my friend, and listen well. He will tell you His secrets and He will show you many things for you to share with His people. He has assigned you to me and I will continue to be with you. Know this, I will always be by your side."

THE BEGINNING

EPILOGUE

Today, Donnie Lee (a pseudonym for the author whose real name is Don Lucado) still lives in Baltimore and is actively involved in Christian ministry. He travels with his local church doing revival meetings mainly on the lower east coast of the United States. He actively uplifts the church by sharing prophesies and ministering in prayer, healing, and deliverance. He is a regular part of the Full Gospel Temple television program readily seen in an online broadcast and on cable in Tennessee, North Carolina, South Carolina, Georgia, and Kentucky.

He continues to accept invitations to churches and television broadcasts where he shares his many touching "Stories from Heaven", some of which are a part of a 2-CD collection, and any message which the Lord chooses to give him for His people.

Don is also a proud grandfather of two grandchildren and three great grandsons. He is actively involved in their lives and is grateful for God's restoration of his family. He remains unmarried and is still friends with his ex-wife who lives next door to him. Currently, he enjoys creating stories which he hopes to publish one day.

Pat, Don's sister lives in a community close to him in Baltimore.

Wanda died about fifteen years prior to the writing of this story.

Shelby died in 2010. In his later years, Shelby wrote pornography. He liked the night life, women, and he loved drinking to excess on weekends. He died of cancer at age sixty eight.

Elizabeth had remarried a Jewish man and gained a new surname name, Persky. She died in 2001. Don has one half brother, Joseph and one half sister, Sandy, whom he loves to visit when he goes to Virginia.

As a young man, while walking the streets of Pulaski, Don and Shelby saw a dark figure coming out of an alley. It was a drunk covered in filthy clothes, carrying the stench of a one who lived amidst the cesspool of wasted life on the streets. The man asked them for some change. Don recognized the man as Mr. Ray. Shelby know no different. Don gave him 11 cents. The figure walked back into the darkness and that was the last time Don ever saw him again.

∞

Don wants to share some things that he feels that God has shown him. These words are what Don has to say:

> *"When I was fasting this second time around for forty days, God told me some things. God told me that He was really upset with the United States because they are doing the same sins that people were doing in the time of Noah, and in the time of Sodom and Gomorrah. He destroyed them for the same sins and will not allow the United States to get away with the same things. He says that He can no longer allow us to do the things which we are doing. He is holding back his hand because of the kindness we show to the Jewish people. And what Nixon did for the Jewish People. Back when Golda Meir was President of Israel and Israel was at war, nobody would help them. They were going to lose the war and she called Nixon early one morning*

and asked Nixon for military help. As Nixon listened to her talk, he remembered that his mother use to pray all the time. She had told him that one of these days he would help the Jewish people. Here was Golda Meir on the phone asking for his help. Nixon starting crying. He call the people in charge and told them to give her anything that she wanted. That is one reason why God has held His hand back from destroying the United States.

And he showed me other things too.

Nobody really love the United States that much. They put up with us for our money.

I've seen millions of people with sickness and disease all over their bodies. He showed me there would be towns with no living people in it. And the streets of major cities like New York City, will be so full of dead bodies that people won't be able to walk down them. There will be people outside of hospitals trying to get in because they want to get a cure for their bodies. Outside of hospitals, bodies will be piled up two stories high, and people will be climbing on them, trying to get through the windows. Fire departments to; anywhere they got medicine people will be trying to get in. Mothers will be holding their babies climbing on top of dead bodies trying to get in through the windows. The bodies underneath would be rotted and mushy and the mothers would sink down into them.

Trees and grass would be dead too because of the disease and the wrath of God.

People will starve. The only thing to eat will be the live maggots that people would get off of the dead bodies. They'd take them home, wash them, and eat them. I heard a voice say that 'Your supper will be in the oven'. Their supper will be their own babies.

God revealed to me that the American people are very spoiled people, especially when it comes to food. They are so used to eating that they can't go without food. Three days without food and they panic. When these tragedies happen, Americans will want to run to Canada, but Canada will not let them come in.

God says to tell the people who are called by His name, that if they humble themselves and pray and seek for His face and turn from their wicked ways, I will hear them from Heaven and bless the land."

∞

Dear Reader,

I want you to know that you are special to God. Before you were born, He knew you and loved you. And, He has a special purpose for you-plans of good and not evil, to give you a future and a hope. Despite the evil forces that come against you, despite your own rebellious, sinful choices at times, God is ever present and wants only your good. Though you may not see his angels, know that he sends them to work on your behalf, for your good. Most importantly, God desires that you know Him and He has made a way for you to come to Him. That way is Jesus. Give Him you; just as you are. He will give you life abundantly. I pray that, despite my weaknesses, my story gives you hope, impresses upon you the extent of God's great love, and inspires you to draw closer to God and to experience all that He has for you.

Donnie Lee